"As we who are kingdom pilgrims journey out of Eg of post-Christendom Christianity, Stuart Murray invites us to dialogue group and a tradition that has been on this journey for almost five centuries. I'm confident that all who are on this journey will benefit tremendously from this work."

—*Gregory A. Boyd, author of* The Myth of a Christian Nation *and* The Myth of a Christian Religion

"Yes, it is good to be naked. That's a profound concession for a traditional Mennonite. Whether you have been steeped in Anabaptism from birth, as I have, or are just trying to understand a peculiar worldview, you will learn a lot from this study written by an English Anabaptist."

—*James Toews, pastor at Neighbourhood Church, Nanaimo, B.C., and* Mennonite Brethren Herald *columnist*

"In *The Naked Anabaptist*, Stuart Murray lays bare—in clear, simple, vulnerable detail—central themes of radical Anabaptism that have sometimes been obscured by the ethnic and cultural garb of the Mennonite denominational tradition. For anyone eager to learn how Anabaptist theology might be translated cross-culturally—whether within the global Anabaptist fellowship or among renewal movements at the edges of mainstream Christianity—this is an essential book."

—*John D. Roth, Goshen College*

"Stuart Murray offers a compelling exploration of the heart of Anabaptism. For traditional Anabaptists, this book serves as a necessary reminder of a dynamic movement that cannot be claimed by anyone but the Spirit. Anabaptists-at-heart will be encouraged by the recognition that they are not alone. And everyone else will be confronted with a vision that, if taken to heart, has the power to revive the church and change the world."

—*Mark Van Steenwyk, JesusManifesto.com and founder of the Missio Dei community in Minneapolis*

"This book's title is an obvious zinger. And so is the book's message. Stuart Murray offers us the best record and analysis so far of Anabaptism's appeal to seekers of many stripes in post-Christendom societies. A must-read for all Anabaptists: cradled, converted, or still considering."

—*James R. Krabill, Mennonite Mission Network*

"We both heartily endorse *The Naked Anabaptist*. It is encouraging when 'an Anabaptist-by-choice' writes enthusiastically about the strengths of Anabaptist biblical interpretation for the broader evangelical audience. Although the author does not gloss over Anabaptist imperfections of the past, he so clearly highlights the richness of our faith."

—*Ruth & Ron Penner, Evangelical Mennonite Conference pastors*

THE NAKED
ANABAPTIST

Part of the Third Way Collection

THE NAKED ANABAPTIST

The Bare Essentials of a Radical Faith

STUART MURRAY

FOREWORD BY GREGORY A. BOYD

Herald Press
Scottdale, Pennsylvania
Waterloo, Ontario

LIBRARY OF CONGRESS CATALOGING-IN-PUBLICATION DATA
Murray, Stuart, 1956-
The naked Anabaptist : the bare essentials of a radical faith / Stuart Murray ; foreword by Gregory A. Boyd.
    p. cm.
ISBN 978-0-8361-9517-0 (pbk. : alk. paper)
1. Anabaptists. I. Title.
BX4931.3.M87 2010
230'.43–dc22

                                                            2010007333

This North American edition of *The Naked Anabaptist* is based on the version first published in 2010 by Paternoster, an imprint of Authentic, 9 Holdom Avenue, Bletchley, Milton Keynes, MK1 1QR, U.K. This edition is published by agreement with Paternoster. In relation to the UK edition, the right of Stuart Murray to be identified as the Author of this Work has been asserted by him in accordance with the Copyright, Designs, and Patents Act 1988.

THE NAKED ANABAPTIST
Copyright © 2010 by Herald Press, Scottdale, PA 15683
  Released simultaneously in Canada by Herald Press,
  Waterloo, Ont. N2L 6H7. All rights reserved
Library of Congress Control Number: 2010007333
International Standard Book Number: 978-0-8361-9517-0
Printed in the United States of America
Cover by Merrill Miller

15 14 13 12 11   10 9 8 7 6 5 4 3

To order or request information please call 1-800-245-7894 or visit www.heraldpress.com.

CONTENTS

FOREWORD

IT IS becoming undeniably clear that western civilization has entered a post-Christian age. Whereas Christians once believed the world would eventually be brought within the expanding empire of Christendom, it is now obvious this will never happen. To the contrary, Christendom has been losing its influence on western culture for several hundred years. Even in America, Christendom's last remaining fortress, the conquest mentality of the "church militant and triumphant" is waning. Undoubtedly, a cultural vestige of the once mighty empire of Christendom will continue for some time in Europe and America, if only in the form of lingering innocuous elements of a Christian civic religion. But for all intents and purposes, the "church militant and triumphant" has become an artifact of history.

While many western Christians understandably are grieved and distressed over this loss, growing choruses of Jesus-followers are viewing it as something to celebrate. I include myself among this rising tribe, as does Stuart Murray, the author of this book.

It's not that we are in any sense pleased with the morally bankrupt form of secularism that has replaced Christendom's reign in the West. It's just that we believe the "church militant and triumphant" bore little resemblance to the church God established through the life, death, and resurrection of Jesus. And now, having left the Egypt of Christendom, we must prepare ourselves for a long and difficult journey in the wilderness.

There is an increasingly shared conviction that the kingdom of God we are called to is radically different from all versions of the kingdoms of the world. While the kingdoms of the world all manifest the character of Caesar as they seek to rule people and conquer enemies with the power of the sword, the kingdom of God always manifests the character of Jesus, seeking to serve people and love enemies as it manifests the power of the cross. The movement Jesus inaugurated is, by its very nature, a counter-cultural, anti-empire

9

movement. More and more followers of Jesus are coming to understand this distinction and to understand that our allegiance to God's kingdom must subvert all other allegiances.

While the mainstream church has, to a significant degree, unwittingly absorbed the values of intense individualism, consumerism, and materialism, more and more post-Christendom disciples in the West are becoming convinced that these values are at odds with everything Jesus was about. They are realizing that we are called to live in community with others, to live simply, humbly, and justly, and to share our lives and our resources with one another and with all who are in need.

What many of those who are journeying in the wilderness of post-Christendom Christianity don't yet realize is that their rejection of Christendom and their insights into the counter-cultural nature of God's kingdom are hardly new. In fact, the vision of the kingdom these tribes are espousing was the general understanding of the church for the first three centuries of its existence. It was quickly exchanged for the model of the "church militant and triumphant" in the fourth century, when Emperor Constantine endowed the church with political power and the church tragically accepted it. Still, throughout the church's history, there have been pockets of Jesus-followers who, despite fierce persecution from the institutional church, held fast to the vision of the kingdom that's arising among post-Christendom Christians today.

The most significant historic expression of the anti-Christendom, Jesus-looking kingdom began during the Reformation among a group of radicals who came to be known as the Anabaptists. Though they often had to pay for it with their lives, this group set itself apart from other reforming movements by espousing the very values the rising tribe of kingdom people is espousing today.

This group was passionate in its conviction that the kingdom of God is radically distinct from the kingdom of the world—and that these two must always be kept distinct. They quickly came to the conclusion that following Jesus requires us to love our enemies and to refuse to resort to violence. They believed that all followers of Jesus are called to live in committed communities with one another as we together cultivate a lifestyle characterized by simplicity, humility, generosity, and a passion for justice. And they were convinced that salvation was not primarily about getting people to heaven when they die but was about God's transforming power affecting every area of life, society, and creation.

Though Christendom's leaders tortured and executed almost all leaders of the Anabaptist movement, by the grace of God the movement survived and has borne witness to God's uniquely beautiful kingdom for the past five hundred years.

As we who are kingdom pilgrims journey out of Egypt through the wilderness of post-Christendom Christianity, Murray invites us to dialogue with a group and a tradition that has been on this journey for almost five centuries. In this book you will find a clear and succinct outline of core Anabaptist beliefs and practices, presented in dialogue with the rising tribes of post-Christendom Jesus-followers today. In true Anabaptist fashion, Murray candidly acknowledges the shortcomings of this tradition along with its strengths.

If one is looking for an unblemished, utopian expression of the kingdom, one will not find it in *The Naked Anabaptist* (or anywhere else). Murray offers this dialogue not to try to get people to join the Mennonites or any other Anabaptist group but simply because it's to the advantage of both Anabaptists and the rising tribe of kingdom people to learn from and support one another. Indeed, from a kingdom perspective, it's *imperative* that we learn from and support one another.

I'm confident that all who have begun to make their way out of the Egypt of Christendom and into the wilderness of post-Christendom Christianity will benefit tremendously from this work. And my prayer is that God will use the dialogue this book begins to advance the beautiful, servant-like, Jesus-looking kingdom throughout the world.

—*Gregory A. Boyd*
Author of The Myth of a Christian Nation
and The Myth of a Christian Religion

ACKNOWLEDGMENTS

I AM grateful to several members of the Anabaptist Network who participated in the writing of this book. Some of their reflections appear in the first two chapters. Others read part or all of the text and gave me some perceptive feedback.

My wife, Sian, also read the whole text, encouraged me to add pictures and more stories, and in other ways improved what I had written. I am very grateful to her for this—and so much else.

Doug Hynd and Tim Nafziger offered helpful comments from Australia and the United States, respectively. And I am especially grateful to Alan Kreider, who read the entire manuscript and whose suggestions have significantly sharpened the text and saved me from errors; any that remain are my responsibility. I also am grateful to Noel Moules for the excellent title.

Disappointingly, though, none of my colleagues accepted the invitation to pose for the front cover.

Introducing "The Naked Anabaptist"

TRAVELING through Pennsylvania in the spring of 2008 with a group of Mennonite church leaders, my friend Noel Moules was quizzed about the growing interest in Anabaptism in Britain and Ireland. Some of these American Mennonites had been in Britain a few weeks earlier and had encountered Christians from various traditions who were deeply attracted to Anabaptist values and insights. They found them intriguing. Why were British and Irish Christians interested in Anabaptism?

The sixteenth-century Anabaptist movement (to which Mennonites and other Anabaptist communities in America trace their origins) had left its mark on various parts of Europe—Switzerland, Austria, Germany, the Netherlands, and the Czech Republic—but very few Anabaptists reached Britain. Those that made it to London in 1575, seeking refuge from persecution elsewhere, were arrested and imprisoned, and either executed or expelled by the authorities. For the next four centuries, although *Anabaptist* was sometimes used as a term of abuse in Britain, there were almost no actual Anabaptists in the country.

So why, Noel was asked, was there a burgeoning Anabaptist movement in Britain and Ireland? What was attracting Christians to a tradition that has no historical roots in their culture? And what does it mean to be an Anabaptist in Britain or Ireland today? What does Anabaptism look like without the Mennonite, Hutterite, or Amish culture in which it is usually clothed in North America?

"Ah, you mean 'the naked Anabaptist,' do you?" asked Noel. "Anabaptism stripped down to the bare essentials." And so this book was born.

Noel and I are both founding members and trustees of the Anabaptist Network in Britain and Ireland. Since the early 1990s, the Anabaptist Network has provided resources for Christians interested in the Anabaptist tradition—study groups, conferences, a journal, newsletters, a theology forum, and an extensive website.[1] For some years we had been concerned that there was no straightforward introduction to Anabaptism easily accessible in Britain and Ireland, written specifically about Anabaptism in that context. There were academic tomes, and books written for the American market, but these were not what we needed to answer questions we are often asked:

- What is an Anabaptist?
- Where did Anabaptism come from?
- What do Anabaptists believe?
- Can I become an Anabaptist?
- What is the difference between Anabaptists and Mennonites?

If you are asking any of these questions, The Naked Anabaptist *is for you.*

So Noel and I agreed with our colleagues in the Anabaptist Network that I would make use of his memorable phrase and write this book. My own encounter with Anabaptism has been told elsewhere.[2] Since the early 1980s, I have identified myself as an Anabaptist, not because I belong to an Anabaptist church or come from an Anabaptist family, but because this is the Christian tradition with which I have by far the greatest theological and spiritual affinity. *The Naked Anabaptist* is, then, at one level an extended personal testimony written by a British Anabaptist to explain his Anabaptist convictions. As such, I will use "I" language from time to time, as in this introduction. But this book was also commissioned by the steering group of the Anabaptist Network, several of whom have contributed to it. And those who receive the Network's newsletters have known for some time about this project. Some of their contributions have also been incorporated. So I have used "we" language in various places to indicate that I am writing on behalf of a community. Sometimes "we" refers to those who have shaped the Network over the past two decades and who would, like me, identify themselves as Anabaptists. Sometimes "we" refers to the wider community of Christians in Britain and Ireland who might not identify themselves as Anabaptists but who belong to the Anabaptist Network and draw gratefully on the Anabaptist tradition. I recognize that this use of language is imprecise, but that is the nature of the Anabaptist movement in Britain and Ireland.

My hope is that this book will be useful, not only to members of the Anabaptist Network who want to explain to their friends why they are intrigued and inspired by Anabaptism and not only to people from other Christian traditions or no Christian tradition who have stumbled across the Anabaptist tradition, but also to North American Anabaptists asking the kinds of questions Noel was asked in Pennsylvania.

I have visited North America many times in the past fifteen years, teaching in Mennonite seminaries, preaching in Mennonite churches, working with Mennonite mission agencies, and speaking at conferences with delegates from Mennonite, Mennonite Brethren, Brethren in Christ, Church of the Brethren, and other denominations descended from the Anabaptists. I have encountered the same incredulity and interest as Noel found in Pennsylvania: why are Christians in Britain and Ireland getting excited about their Anabaptist forebears?

This question is given added poignancy by the *lack* of interest in the Anabaptist tradition among many North American Mennonites. I have often found myself urging Mennonite students and church leaders to recover their own radical heritage as a source of renewal and inspiration. Although Mennonite scholars during the twentieth century embarked on a quest to rehabilitate Anabaptism, their passion and insights have not yet had the impact they deserve. Many Mennonites seem more interested in purpose-driven churches or the Alpha course.

Maybe Mennonite culture and traditions have stifled the Anabaptist heritage. Some years ago I had a conversation with a leader of a large youth organization who reported that at a recent staff conference they had received a word that they regarded as prophetic: "Let go of your traditions and hold on to your heritage." She and her colleagues were pondering the implications of this challenge, recognizing that many traditions had grown up over the years that might have been valuable once but were now hindering the organization from fulfilling its primary calling. *If you recognize this in your own North American Anabaptist-related tradition,* The Naked Anabaptist *is for you.*

It is not only in Britain and Ireland that Christians from diverse backgrounds are appropriating the Anabaptist tradition. There are Anabaptist centers in Korea, Japan, and South Africa. There is an Anabaptist Association in Australia and New Zealand, and a new Anabaptist Network is emerging in Scandinavia. None of these nations have any historic Anabaptist connections. There is also a new Francophone Anabaptist center in Montreal. In North America, too, where Mennonite, Hutterite, Amish, and other Anabaptist groups are part of the cultural and religious environment, Christians from other denominations (including evangelical and emerging networks) are discovering the Anabaptist tradition. Some are now identifying themselves as Anabaptists; others are urging the Mennonites to value more highly their own heritage and to recognize its contemporary significance.[3]

And in academic circles, after centuries of neglect, marginalization, and caricature, there is growing interest in Anabaptism way beyond the Mennonite community. I am currently supervising two doctoral students working on Anabaptism. One is from Korea; the other is a French Canadian who has been church planting in Belgium and is now teaching in Rwanda. And the Anabaptist Network website frequently receives emails from students writing essays or dissertations on Anabaptism, asking for advice and resources.

In many nations, then, not only in Britain and Ireland, there are growing numbers of *neo-Anabaptists* and *hyphenated Anabaptists.* Neo-Anabaptists identify with the Anabaptist tradition and are happy to be known as Anabaptists, but have no historic or cultural links with any Anabaptist-related denomination. Hyphenated Anabaptists find inspiration and resources in the Anabaptist tradition, but do not identify themselves as Anabaptists. They might be Baptist-Anabaptists, Methodist-Anabaptists, Anglican-Anabaptists, Pentecostal-Anabaptists, or various other combinations. *If you identify with either of these designations,* The Naked Anabaptist *is for you.*

In 1953, the London Mennonite Centre was established, bringing an Anabaptist presence back into Britain for the first time in nearly four hundred years.[4] Its influence gradually permeated British and Irish churches, encouraging Christians from many backgrounds to reflect afresh on issues of community, peace, justice, and discipleship. But only in the 1980s did the term *Anabaptism* begin to be used more widely, and it is even more recently that the Anabaptist movement has really become visible.

In 2004, the first book in the After Christendom series was published by Paternoster Press. This series (all published in the United Kingdom) is an initiative of the Anabaptist Network steering group, which has invited various authors to reflect on the implications of the end of the Christendom era in many western societies, drawing on Anabaptist perspectives. By 2009, five books had been published, and others are currently being written or are awaiting publication. *Post-Christendom*, published in 2004,[5] celebrated the demise of imperial Christianity and welcomed the opportunity to rethink all kinds of issues as the European church found itself back on the margins of society. It suggested that, as the mainline traditions associated with imperial Christianity struggled to adjust to this new situation, perhaps some of the necessary resources are to be found in the radical tradition associated with Anabaptism. Could it be, as some have suggested, that Anabaptism is "a vision whose time has come"? The After Christendom series, which has been widely read and enthusiastically received, has introduced many others to this tradition.

So, all over the place, Christians (and others) in Britain and Ireland (and elsewhere) are bumping into Anabaptists. But who are these people? What do they believe? What practices do they have in common with other Christians, and what are their distinctives? Why have they suddenly emerged in post-Christendom western societies? And can you really be an Anabaptist without living in a common-purse community like the Hutterites, driving a buggy like the Amish, or belonging to a Mennonite church and singing in four-part harmony? *If you've encountered Anabaptists and want to know more about them,* The Naked Anabaptist *is for you.*

Welcome to *The Naked Anabaptist!*

1

Uncovering Anabaptists

ANABAPTISTS ALL OVER THE PLACE

"The Anabaptists are back!" announced an American author a few years ago in a book with this title.[1] He was intrigued by growing interest in the Anabaptist tradition in North America, where Mennonite, Hutterite, and Amish communities have long been part of the religious scene. Christians from many other traditions were discovering the practices and convictions of these quiet, often withdrawn, communities—and finding them surprisingly relevant in contemporary culture. Something similar seems to have been happening in Britain and Ireland. Anabaptists are becoming visible in a society where, unlike North America, they had not been part of the religious scene until very recently.

The Anabaptist Network was launched in 1991 to serve Christians from many churches and denominations in the United Kingdom who had stumbled across Anabaptism and wanted more resources and opportunities to learn together. During the past twenty years, many others have joined the Network or have contacted us with comments or questions that have become familiar:

- "I'm so relieved to find others who believe what I do. People in my church think I'm crazy when I go on about these things."
- "You Anabaptists seem to be popping up all over the place."
- "What is an Anabaptist?"
- "What do Anabaptists think about . . . ?"
- "Where is the nearest Anabaptist church to me?"

Our first attempt to respond to this interest and answer these questions was a collection of stories, published in 2000 under the title *Coming Home: Stories of Anabaptists in Britain and Ireland*.[2] Anabaptism is a story-rich tradition, so presenting the stories of about sixty Christians who identified with the Anabaptist tradition seemed appropriate. These stories recount how the contributors discovered Anabaptism and what attracted them.

The "coming home" theme emerged so often in these stories that it became the title of the book. It was not that the Anabaptists were "back"—there had hardly been any Anabaptists in Britain and Ireland for the past four centuries—but those who discovered Anabaptism experienced this encounter, as I did, as a homecoming. Here were other Christians who shared our convictions about discipleship, community, peace, and mission.

In the past few years, Anabaptists have become even more visible—and vocal. We have continued to organize conferences and study groups in different parts of the country, but there is also now a consortium of a dozen or more "Anabaptist-flavored" organizations involved in all kinds of activities, ranging from church planting to training programs; conflict transformation to media work; restorative justice and peacemaking to a political think tank. And we have received invitations to contribute "an Anabaptist perspective" in books and conversations on various subjects, including church and state, the atonement, diaconal ministry, the Alpha course, and the emerging church.

Surprisingly for a tradition routinely accused of being sectarian, interest in Anabaptism today is remarkably ecumenical and boundary crossing. On the Network's website are stories of Christians from several denominations who have been "drawn to Anabaptism." Although many are from evangelical backgrounds, Christians from liberal, charismatic, Reformed, and Anglo-Catholic backgrounds are represented in the Network. Writers from many traditions have spoken warmly of Anabaptism, some suggesting it might be a movement whose time has come and a way of being Christian that makes sense in post-Christendom culture. This strange ecumenism is worrying to some, but deeply attractive to others.

We have also noticed in recent years that a number of people attending our conferences have had no recent church connection. Indeed, some would not call themselves Christians at all. I had a conversation at a recent event with an anarchist who was fascinated by the Anabaptist tradition. And one of the stories on the website was written by an ex-atheist ex-Buddhist, who has found through Anabaptism an authentic Christian faith.

So when we hear that Anabaptists are "popping up all over the place," we understand why some might think this. But the Anabaptist tradition is still very much a minority voice in Britain and Ireland. Some of us are happy to be known as "Anabaptists," but many others resist this tag and prefer to talk about the positive impact of Anabaptism on their thinking and practice as Catholics, Baptists, Methodists, or whatever. A very small number of local churches identify themselves explicitly as Anabaptist, but several others have embraced Anabaptist values and introduced Anabaptist processes and resources.

So, if Anabaptists are all over the place, we are spread pretty thinly in Britain and Ireland, and we are often not that obvious. This may explain the diverse comments and questions we receive from some who are relieved to find us and from others who are surprised we exist. There is more chance now of uncovering Anabaptists, in person or in print, but who are we and what do we believe? *The Naked Anabaptist* is an attempt to answer these questions.

BUMPING INTO ANABAPTISTS

For those in the Europe, where might you already have bumped into Anabaptists? You might have attended one of the conferences the Anabaptist Network has organized in the past two decades—not necessarily because the event was organized by Anabaptists, but because you were interested in the subject matter. Topics have included learning from the early church, the implications of the end of Christendom, gender issues, worship and mission, English radicalism, the practice of community, becoming a peace church, faith and politics, why people are leaving the church, radical discipleship, youth ministry, and new monasticism. Three conferences, cosponsored with the Northumbria Community, have explored the contributions of the Anabaptist and Celtic traditions to contemporary discipleship.

You might have come across *Coming Home*, the book of stories mentioned above, or a copy of *Anabaptism Today*, the journal we published for several years until 2004. You might have recognized someone featured in one of the stories or the author of one of the articles and thought, *I didn't know that person was an Anabaptist!*

More recently you might have thumbed through, or even sat down and read properly, one of the books in the After Christendom series, mentioned in the introduction.[3] Perhaps you did not know enough about Anabaptism to spot Anabaptist perspectives permeating these books, but some reviewers did—one of them commenting on the "Anabaptist axe grinding in the background."

You might have encountered Anabaptist perspectives on international events through *On the Road*, the journal of the Anabaptist Association of Australia and New Zealand.[4]

You might have been to one of only two Mennonite churches in England: the Wood Green Mennonite Church in North London or the recently planted Portuguese-speaking and mainly Brazilian Mennonite church in Eastbourne. Or you might have been in touch with other Anabaptist-influenced churches, such as Peace Church in Birmingham, the E1 Community Church in East London, or the Wesleyan Reformed Church in Mexborough.

You might have come across one of two common-purse communities in the southeast of England (in Kent or Sussex), known as Bruderhofs. Drawing inspiration from one branch of the Anabaptist movement—the Hutterites, who have lived in community for centuries—Bruderhof communities offer a distinctive and radical expression of certain Anabaptist values and practices.[5]

You might have read about the tragic shooting of Amish school children in Nickel Mines, Pennsylvania, in October 2006—and the startling response of this Anabaptist community as it expressed forgiveness toward the gunman and reached out in compassion toward his family. Or you might have been aware of the Amish already if you saw the 1985 film *The Witness*, starring Harrison Ford and Kelly McGillis. But you may have associated this community with buggies and bonnets, and not with Anabaptism.

You may remember Norman Kember and his colleagues, held hostage in Iraq, where they were members of a Christian Peacemaker Team. You may not know that this organization was founded in response to a challenge at an Anabaptist gathering in 1984 to go beyond pacifism to costly peacemaking: "What would happen if Christians devoted the same discipline and self-sacrifice to nonviolent peacemaking that armies devote to war?"[6]

You might have encountered Mennonite volunteers in Northern Ireland at the height of "the troubles" there, working quietly as agents of reconciliation in a divided community, and training others in nonviolent approaches to conflict.

You might have stumbled across Anabaptists through the work of Urban Expression, an inner-city church-planting agency, founded in 1997, which is working in several British cities and now also in the Netherlands and North America.[7] Although not an explicitly Anabaptist mission agency, it has Anabaptist values at its core, as several observers have commented. Urban Expression is one of the main sponsors of the Crucible course.[8]

You might have been in a conflict transformation training program run by Bridge Builders, based at the London Mennonite Centre, which has trained hundreds of church leaders from various denominations.[9] You might have ordered books on discipleship, peace, or community from the Metanoia Book Service, another of the center's services.[10] You might have visited the center for one of its Cross Currents seminars or "table talks," or noticed its stand at the Greenbelt Festival.

You might have studied with the Workshop Christian training program,[11] which has run for over a quarter of a century in cities across Britain. As you listened to its director, Noel Moules, teaching on different subjects each month, you might have begun to recognize a distinctive approach to church, mission, the Bible, discipleship, and community. Perhaps only toward the end of the year did you realize that Noel and many other teachers on the course were Anabaptists, even if they rarely used this label.

You might have been puzzled or intrigued by statements from Jonathan Bartley or Simon Barrow, directors of the Christian political think tank Ekklesia.[12] In media interviews, in articles on their website, and in daily comments on the news, they offer perspectives on church, theology, ethics, politics, economics, culture, education, or global issues that often challenge familiar Christian assumptions and priorities. You might not have realized that both have been strongly influenced by the Anabaptist tradition.

You might have participated in days of action initiated by Speak,[13] a network connecting young adults and students to campaign and pray about issues of global injustice. Some years ago, members of Speak and members of the Anabaptist Network discovered each other and recognized shared values. One of Speak's leaders, Jo Frew, remembers: "Anabaptism is something we found out about and thought, 'Yeah, that seems like us!'"

If you are an Anglican, you might have discovered a surprising (and negative) reference to Anabaptists in the founding document of the Church of England. Although there were practically no Anabaptists in the country, fear of this continental movement prompted the inclusion of the thirty-eighth of the *Thirty-Nine Articles of Religion* (1571), which warns English Christians about this worrying movement.[14]

If you are a Baptist, and especially if you took part in the celebrations in July 2009 that marked the four-hundredth anniversary of the start of the Baptist movement, you might know that English Baptist refugees first met in an Anabaptist baker's shop in Amsterdam and that early Baptist leaders were deeply influenced by Dutch Anabaptists. You may not know that Baptist historians continue to debate whether Anabaptism should be acknowledged as the source (or at least one major source) of the Baptist movement.

If you are (or have been in the past few years) a student at any of the Baptist colleges in England and Wales, you have probably encountered at least one tutor who is a member of the Anabaptist Network. At Spurgeon's College in London and also at the International Baptist Theological Seminary in Prague, you would have had the opportunity to take courses or modules in Anabaptist studies. And if you were a student at Bristol University in the past two or three years, you might have participated in one of the first modules on Anabaptism to be taught in a British university.

If you have been involved in the New Churches (previously known as the House Church movement), you might have encountered Roger Forster (the founder of Ichthus Christian Fellowship) introducing Anabaptists in his church history course as one of several radical movements that continue to inspire Christians today.

If you participate in the "emerging church conversation," you are probably aware of Brian McLaren's writings. His book *A Generous Orthodoxy*[15] includes Anabaptism as one of the traditions he values. Elsewhere he writes, "Anabaptists know things that all of us need as we slide or run or crawl or are dragged into the postmodern world."[16] He suggested in a recent interview, "Emergent represents a rediscovery of the Anabaptist spirit. It's very hard in other Protestant denominations to find people who take Jesus as teacher deeply seriously, and take Jesus' teachings and the Sermon on the Mount, and Jesus' example of nonviolence, seriously."[17]

If you are interested in church history, especially in the Reformation era in Europe (early sixteenth century), you may have encountered references to the Anabaptists as a "third way" that was neither Catholic nor Protestant. If you studied some time ago, these might have been only passing references or footnotes. If there was more, it might well have been an account of the reign of terror a renegade band of Anabaptists imposed on the city of Münster in the mid-1530s. Most church history textbooks and courses now offer a more balanced treatment of early Anabaptist history, but old caricatures still appear in unexpected places (including *Third Way* magazine and Spring Harvest teaching notes in recent years).

If you are interested in theology or ethics, you may have read books or articles by Stanley Hauerwas, James McClendon, or John Howard Yoder. Hauerwas is an Episcopalian who teaches at a Methodist university, McClendon was a Baptist, and Yoder was a Mennonite, but all three drank deeply of the Anabaptist tradition, and their writings reflect this.[18]

If cooking and hospitality appeal to you more than theology and ethics, you might have encountered Anabaptism without realizing it in various cookbooks, especially the *More-with-Less Cookbook* by a Mennonite, Doris Janzen Longacre.[19] When we invited people to tell their stories in *Coming Home*, we asked which books (if any) had introduced them to Anabaptism. The top two were John Howard Yoder's *The Politics of Jesus* and the *More-with-Less Cookbook*.

If you are interested in art, you might be aware that Rembrandt painted a portrait of the Mennonite preacher Cornelis Claesz Anslo and his wife, and had links with the Mennonites in the seventeenth century. Indeed, some even suspected Rembrandt of being an Anabaptist himself—almost certainly wrongly, though he was undoubtedly sympathetic to the movement.

If you are involved in the criminal justice system, you are probably familiar with efforts to incorporate "restorative justice" principles alongside the dominant retributive approach. You may not know that Anabaptists were pioneers of this alternative approach, especially through victim-offender reconciliation programs.[20]

If you have vacationed in Europe and enjoy visiting historic sites, you might have read in your guide book about Anabaptist communities and incidents in early Anabaptist history—not just in Münster, but also in Zürich, Strasbourg, Amsterdam, and several other cities. You might even have found the guided walk on the Anabaptist Network website that takes you around several sites in central London that have links with Anabaptism and other radical groups.

Where have you bumped into Anabaptists before reading this book?

ENCOUNTERING ANABAPTISM

When I began writing this book, I invited people involved in the Anabaptist Network to tell me, as succinctly as they could, how they had encountered Anabaptism and how the tradition had impacted them. Here are some of their responses:

I encountered Anabaptism during a time when I was trying desperately to inhabit very different worlds: the ungrounded world of charismatic spirituality; the intense intellectual world of theology; and the daily struggle with life where I spent most of my time. Anabaptism brought these together in a holistic way and helped me think, act, and feel my way to God.
—*Tim Foley (Portadown, Northern Ireland)*

Discovering Anabaptism was like finding the edge bits of a jigsaw puzzle. We were already attempting to piece together a thoughtful lifestyle and a commitment to Christian community while paying global attention and grappling with Scripture. Then we met people further along this same journey and found a satisfying mix of honesty and fun.

—*Bill and Ali Phelps (Leeds, England)*

I first came across Anabaptism via people at the New Churches' Theology Forum. I quickly discovered that Anabaptist teaching and practice resonated with ways of being church that were foundational to the church I belong to, though our attempts seemed feeble compared to the cost they paid for their discipleship.

—*Linda Wilson (Bristol, England)*

I'd always felt uncomfortable with all forms of "civic religion." I felt instinctively that Christians should not be ruling society but should be a witness to it, an alternative society with different values. I'd also been unhappy with Christian attempts to recall society to standards, such as the Ten Commandments, and wondered what had happened to the revolution of Jesus. I felt followers of Christ had to be more than moralists. I didn't understand how anyone could approve of war from a Christian perspective. And I longed for community, not just "fellowship," in the church. When I discovered Anabaptism, I found I'd really been an Anabaptist all along without knowing it. The church to me is not the glue of the establishment, but an outpost of the radical changes the kingdom brings.

—*Veronica Zundel (London)*

My family background is in the Churches of Christ, an Anabaptist movement. I understood church needed to be a voluntary, multivoiced community of baptized believers. What made Anabaptism decisive is its emphasis on "following after" the way and words of Jesus: peace-giving, thirst-quenching, disciplemaking, earth-sharing, risk-taking faith.

—*Andrew Francis (Swindon, England)*

I discovered G. H. Williams's *The Radical Reformation* at the university in the early 1970s: it revolutionized my study and teaching. The unjust exclusion of Anabaptists from the history offended me, and their radical interrogation of Christian tradition and practice challenged me—in a historic denomination—to take nothing in my church for granted.

—*Adrian Chatfield (Cambridge, England)*

I came across Anabaptism through Urban Expression, and it was attractive
as it seemed to be voicing things that I was feeling instinctively. It was great
to find a group of people who thought similar things to me and to be able to
think more deeply about these things.

—*Sarah Warburton (London)*

Our backgrounds are Baptist and Brethren, and exploring the Anabaptist
tradition has provided us with a place of spiritual "common ground." We have
particularly related to the emphasis on peace, justice, and radical discipleship,
and have found our local Anabaptist Network group to be a place of community
and accountability.

—*Simon and Liz Woodman (Bristol, England)*

I was increasingly disillusioned by the kind of evangelicalism that joined the dots
between faith and political conservatism. Talking with the director of the London
Mennonite Centre in the early 1980s, I remember we talked about simplicity,
community, and peacemaking, but it was the "feel" of the day that remains with
me: the sense that I had found a place of belonging and integration.

—*Phil Wood (Wallingford, England)*

Conversion doesn't always happen in the comfort of churches full of
knowledgeable people. Life afterwards is never easy, dealing with past
sins. The honesty of Anabaptists helped me take Jesus' words at face value
with no extras, and to love and accept myself; so important before you can
love others.

—*Pete Jones (Liverpool, England)*

I first encountered the Anabaptists as a child due to my father's interest in
their history and theology. I renewed my interest in this tradition as an adult,
partly in response to a crisis of faith but mainly due to dissatisfaction with
modern theology and church-growth models.

—*David Kirkman (Annan, Scotland)*

The recovery of Anabaptist emphases on discipleship, church as subversive
and exemplary community, the biblical word oriented toward Jesus the
living word, and peacemaking as integral to the gospel has given me fresh

hope for a truly liberating, post-Christendom vision and practice of Christianity—something both committed and open.

—*Simon Barrow (Exeter, England)*

My encounter with the Anabaptist tradition has radically changed my attitude to peace, the gospel, and the course of my life. It has led me to leave a job in which I felt unable to truly embrace Jesus' nonviolence and call to peace; it has led me to investigate ways of sharing an Anabaptist understanding of peace with other people in the church; and it has led me to apply to be part of a delegation to Colombia with Christian Peacemaker Teams—to see for myself how people living with and threatened by violence are responding nonviolently.

—*Ros Parkes (Bristol, England)*

BUT AREN'T ANABAPTISTS . . . ?

Some of those who bump into Anabaptists, past or present, in print or in person, have no preconceived ideas about a tradition that is quite new to them. For others, Anabaptism may have various associations—some positive, others quaint, and a few rather disturbing. As nakedness implies vulnerability, it seems appropriate, early in *The Naked Anabaptist*, to uncover some of the charges against Anabaptists.

If Anabaptism is new to you and you have not heard disturbing things about Anabaptists, you can, of course, skip this section—unless you want to know what kinds of things they have often been accused of or associated with.

But aren't Anabaptists just a footnote in church history? What relevance does a bunch of sixteenth-century troublemakers have today?

It is certainly true that, until quite recently, students reading standard textbooks on church history encountered the Anabaptists, if at all, as a footnote to the main action. In the first half of the sixteenth century, the Catholic Church and the Protestant reformers occupied center stage, competing for hearts and minds and, at least as importantly, for the support of various political authorities. When the dust finally settled, western Europe had been divided into Catholic and Protestant zones, and citizens in each zone were expected to concur with the religious choices their rulers had made.

Anabaptists faced serious difficulties in both Catholic and Protestant zones; they were persecuted because they refused to submit to the demands of the state churches and conform to the beliefs and practices of their superiors. They were, indeed, regarded as troublemakers who were teaching heretical ideas, setting up unauthorized churches, calling people to be baptized as followers of Jesus, questioning the legitimacy of violence and wealth, and in other ways disturbing the status quo. Unlike Catholic and Protestant Christians, they had no zones of their own where they could practice their faith unhindered. Occasionally, if a landowner or prince was sympathetic, they found temporary refuge, but imperial pressure soon forced him to expel or arrest them.

Their contemporaries wavered between dismissing the Anabaptists as a minor irritant and damning them as dangerous heretics, writing at length about their deviant behavior. Occasionally, extreme elements among the Anabaptists—persecution sometimes leads to extremism—played into their hands. Most notorious was an incident in 1534-35, when some Anabaptists gained control of the North German city of Münster and, convinced that the return of Christ was imminent, instituted a reign of terror designed to cleanse the city and prepare it for this great event. The city was besieged by a Catholic army, its inhabitants were massacred, and the bodies of the rebel leaders were displayed in cages as a warning to others. Most Anabaptists denounced this tragic episode as contravening fundamental Anabaptist principles, but Protestant and Catholic authorities across Europe pointed to Münster as proof that this supposedly peaceful movement was dangerous.

Historians have oscillated between consigning Anabaptism to a footnote and telling the story of Münster as if it were typical of the movement. Another unsavory incident, sometimes also reported as representative, was a naked procession in Amsterdam to warn of coming judgment (not the kind of "naked Anabaptism" we have in mind).

Until quite recently, historians generally endorsed the judgments of those who were opposed to the Anabaptists. They either treated

Anabaptists as marginal or presented them in a very negative light. What few historians did was to investigate what Anabaptists wrote or said about themselves or how most Anabaptists actually lived.

Only in the past half century have historians begun to take Anabaptism more seriously as a radical renewal movement that might have considerable contemporary significance. At first, Mennonite historians led the way as they scoured their past for resources for faithful discipleship today. Others have joined them, from different Christian traditions and from none. They have translated Anabaptist tracts and treatises, collected and analyzed records of Anabaptists on trial, told the stories of individuals and communities, traced the social and geographical spread of the movement, and shown that Münster and naked processions were *atypical*. Their interpretations and assessments of Anabaptism have varied, but there is no longer any justification for marginalizing the movement or judging it on the basis of its worst moments.

Renewed interest in the Anabaptist tradition owes much to the careful research of these scholars. And the rediscovery of Anabaptism is timely. As the Christendom era comes to an end and the mainstream Catholic and Protestant traditions that were victorious in the sixteenth-century struggle to adjust to a changing culture, the alternative perspectives of the long-neglected Anabaptist tradition (which rejected Christendom as a wrong turn in European church history) suddenly seem attractive and highly relevant. Perhaps they were not just a bunch of sixteenth-century troublemakers who should be consigned to obscurity, but a prophetic movement whose voices we need to hear today.

One of the obstacles we face as we investigate this tradition is that Anabaptism is sometimes presented in a rather academic way. Maybe this is not surprising, given the role of scholars and historians in recovering Anabaptism. But most recent directors of the London Mennonite Centre (where many of us discovered the Anabaptists) have also been academics. And interest in Anabaptism in Britain and Ireland over the past twenty years has perhaps been strongest among church leaders and tutors at theological colleges.

There is a danger that Anabaptism can be regarded as a special-interest group for historians and other academics (or "posh Baptists" as someone recently remarked). This would be a great shame, depriving us of very practical resources for mission, church life, and discipleship in an emerging post-Christendom culture. It would also be untrue to the Anabaptist movement itself, which was overwhelmingly comprised of nonacademic, often uneducated, Christians who were passionate about their faith, resilient in the face of sustained opposition, and extraordinarily irritating to the academics who tried to convince them of their errors. *The Naked Anabaptist* is an attempt to present Anabaptism in a less academic way.

But aren't Anabaptists just another denomination? I'm an Anglican, Methodist, Baptist, Pentecostal . . . (insert your own tribe). Why should I be interested in another tradition?
The Anabaptist movement began as a loose-knit coalition of groups who were forming in various places across central Europe—the sixteenth-century equivalent of the "emerging church." These groups spoke different languages, were shaped by different spiritual and cultural influences, and did not always agree with each other on all aspects of faith and practice. There was a central core of belief and behavior that distinguished them from others and welded them together into a movement, but Anabaptism was never uniform. Nor did it form a single denomination. Driven underground or scattered by persecution, developing denominational structures was neither feasible nor the main priority in the early years. Gradually, institutional features began to emerge, and eventually a number of denominations or distinct groupings developed. In common with many other traditions that broke away from the Catholic Church, Anabaptist denominations subdivided from time to time, and some subsequently reconnected.

The major denominations or communities that trace their origins to Anabaptism are the Mennonites, the Mennonite Brethren, the Hutterites, the Amish, the Brethren in Christ, and the Church of the Brethren. Baptists continue to debate how much they owe their beginnings to the influence of the Anabaptists: there are many shared characteristics and convictions, but also some significant differences. If we exclude the Baptists, as indirect rather than direct descendants of the

Anabaptists, there is virtually no denominational expression of Anabaptism in Britain and Ireland. The interest in Anabaptism reported in this chapter has impacted people from many denominations, but it has not created a new denomination here.

Why are Anglicans, Presbyterians, Catholics, Quakers, Methodists, Baptists, and others interested in the Anabaptist tradition? Most are not searching for a new denomination to join or looking for a way to leave their own. They are seeking inspiration, resources, and fresh perspectives to enrich and enhance their own lives, local church, or denomination, and they suspect that the Anabaptist tradition might have something to offer. Because Anabaptism (especially as people encounter it in Britain and Ireland) is a tradition rather than a denomination, they can explore it and learn from it without feeling disloyal to their own community.

Neither the Anabaptist Network nor the London Mennonite Centre (the two communities in Britain to which people usually go to explore Anabaptism) has attempted to express Anabaptist values and practices by planting churches or founding a new denomination. Both groups have offered resources to Christians from many denominations without suggesting they should abandon their existing commitments. There are advantages to this policy, but we recognize that it also has certain drawbacks—not least that the Anabaptist tradition can be presented in an idealistic or disembodied way that is not tested in the rough-and-tumble of church life and denominational relationships. This is not so much "naked Anabaptism" as ethereal Anabaptism. But with this health warning attached, we continue to invite people from any denomination to take what they find helpful from the Anabaptist tradition.

Anabaptism is not, of course, the only tradition to which people are looking for insights and inspiration today. Many more are looking to Celtic Christianity and finding resources to sustain and renew them. There are fewer historical sources from which we can attempt to discover authentic Celtic Christianity, so the danger of reading back into this tradition what we want to find is greater than with Anabaptism. But people from many traditions embrace Celtic perspectives and practices without disconnecting from their own church or denomination. And the Celtic tradition has been mediated through poetry, art, music, and liturgy, rather than academic presentations, making it more accessible than the Anabaptist tradition.

In an increasingly post-denominational era, and with easy access to resources of all kinds, few Christians today draw only on one tradition or stream of spirituality. While there are undoubtedly dangers in sampling many traditions without inhabiting any and of slipping in and out of communities rather than truly belonging, restrictive tribal loyalties no longer discourage us from learning from others beyond our immediate boundaries. *The Naked Anabaptist* is not suggesting that the Anabaptist stream is the only one we should drink from, but that it has been a less familiar tradition than many others and that learning from it does not threaten other commitments.

But aren't Anabaptists hung up on the issue of baptism?

As has been the case with many other movements, the label "Anabaptist" was imposed by others rather than chosen by the people involved—who tended to call themselves simply Christians or "brothers and sisters." And, as often, the label referred to a distinctive aspect of the movement rather than its central convictions. In the case of the Anabaptists, it was their rejection of infant baptism and their insistence on baptizing believers (even if they had been baptized as infants) that prompted their opponents to label them "Anabaptists" ("rebaptizers").

This was an important and hugely contentious issue in the sixteenth century. Baptizing infants marked their incorporation into a Christian society; rebaptizing them years later implied that they—and the society into which they had been inducted—were not truly Christian. This was precisely what the Anabaptists claimed, causing huge offense in the process. They argued that infant baptism lacked biblical support and disconnected the rite of baptism from the reality of faith and discipleship. Baptism, they taught, was reserved for those who could choose to follow Jesus and commit themselves to the community of the church. But they refused to regard this as *re*baptism, claiming that infant baptism was *no baptism at all*. The label "Anabaptist" was applied to them, not only to challenge this assertion, but to make them liable to prosecution under an ancient law that forbade such rebaptism on pain of execution.

But the distinctive and subversive Anabaptist practice of baptism pointed to deeper issues that the label does not pick up. Baptizing believers and associating this rite with entry into the church challenged the way in which church membership had been understood during the Christendom era. For believers baptism meant a believers church, not a territorial church; entered by choice, not birth; requiring active participation, not just attendance. It also meant that discipleship was not a higher calling for monks and nuns but expected of *all* believers. And it was based on the judgment that biblical precedent trumped ecclesial tradition. No matter how many centuries of baptizing infants the Catholic and Protestant churches could point to in support of this practice, if it lacked a convincing biblical basis, Anabaptists were unimpressed.

These were revolutionary ideas in the sixteenth century, but are hardly so today. Many Christians now (though not all) are willing to question long-established traditions if these appear to be unsupported by Scripture. The believers church model is not only familiar alongside the state church or people's church models but is becoming normative in most societies. And few would now suggest that the call to discipleship is applicable to only a spiritual elite. Questions about baptism may still be contentious, but the Anabaptists have carried the day on the issues to which their baptismal practice pointed.

Furthermore, the cultural context is significantly different today. Some have suggested that in post-Christendom, baptizing one's child is as much an act of spiritual defiance as refusing to baptize one's child was in the sixteenth century. This is not an argument for infant baptism most Anabaptists would find persuasive, but it does highlight the culture shift that requires Christians in all traditions to think carefully about the induction and nurture of children within the Christian community. And it indicates that the cultural significance of infant baptism may be evolving into something different than it has been for many centuries.

Maybe this explains why Anabaptists today are not "hung up on baptism" in the way they seemed to be in the sixteenth century.[21] It is not that baptism is unimportant, but this practice no longer carries the freight it carried before. So those who continue to defend and practice infant baptism can participate freely in Anabaptist gatherings and draw on the Anabaptist tradition without needing to argue about baptismal practice. And those who advocate and practice the baptism of believers can welcome and worship alongside those who disagree with them in a way that would have been unthinkable 450 years ago.

But aren't Anabaptists separatists? Don't Anabaptist communities withdraw from the world and refuse to get involved in society?

There are certainly some Anabaptist communities today that adopt a separatist stance and appear withdrawn from the rest of society. Amish and Hutterite communities, especially, are distinctive in the way they dress and the restrictions they impose on themselves and their engagement with outsiders. These communities regard such separation as essential for faithful discipleship. This may not imply that they are unconcerned for others; indeed, members of these communities have sometimes been actively involved in campaigns for social justice, especially in protesting against the death penalty. But they understand their primary calling to be living out the gospel in their daily lives, in preparation for the age to come, and as a witness to any who will pay attention.

Most other Anabaptists today, whether members of denominations descended from the Anabaptists or others who identify with the Anabaptist tradition, do not subscribe to this understanding of mission or this perspective on separation. But the Anabaptist tradition is dogged by the charge of separatism, which is often made without supporting evidence. In some ways this is understandable, given statements from the early years of the movement that are unmistakably separatist in tone. But these statements need to be read in context. Persecuted communities often have little option but separation if they hope to survive. If the state is trying to eradicate you, if other churches brand you as "heretics" and neighbors are expected to denounce and betray you to the authorities, what else can you do?

In fact, early Anabaptists were deeply concerned about social justice, economic issues, and community transformation. Many had participated in the peasants' movement of the mid-1520s until this was crushed by military force. This experience persuaded them that the only way forward in the current climate was to form separate communities in which they could embody their convictions and from which they could reach out in mission to any who would listen. This led to a wave of church planting across Europe. Anabaptism was, at its core, a missional movement.

But the authorities found these unauthorized churches, their deviant convictions, and their enthusiastic advocates too threatening to ignore. Years of persecution eventually silenced the Anabaptists, who either fled or survived by withdrawing into their own communities and ceasing to talk about their beliefs—in some places they became known as "the quiet in the land." This understandable response to persecution then became embedded in the Anabaptist tradition so that, when persecution ceased, the separatist instinct was hard to resist. Anabaptists have frequently succumbed to withdrawal over the centuries, so the charge of separatism is not without foundation, but this can be interpreted as a distortion of the original vision.

Anabaptists today, with the exceptions mentioned above, interpret separation differently. Some have frankly become assimilated into the wider culture and retain only vestiges of their nonconforming heritage. Others have explored ways of expressing their convictions and distinctives creatively in different cultural contexts. Many have become passionately engaged in social, economic, and political activism, or in evangelistic and church-planting initiatives. The charge of separatism simply does not apply to them. Members of the Anabaptist Network's steering group, for example, cannot legitimately be characterized as separatists. This group includes an inner-city church planter, a social worker, a university lecturer, a staff member of Christian Aid, a psychiatrist, a mediator working on the issue of gang violence, and the CEO of a global environmental agency.

Some years ago, one of us was invited to address a meeting of academic theologians in Cambridge. During the discussion that followed his presentation, he was charged, as an Anabaptist, with advocating withdrawal from the world. Having come straight from his office, where he worked as the financial director of a large business, into the rarefied atmosphere of a theological study center, he found this accusation bizarre and amusing.

The Naked Anabaptist will offer many examples of ways in which Anabaptists today, far from advocating withdrawal, are engaging creatively and courageously in society. It is time for the charge of separatism to be reviewed. And yet, perhaps separatism should not be dropped entirely, and perhaps Anabaptists should insist that a separatist approach is not completely unwarranted. The Old and New Testaments both call for the people of God to be distinctive, nonconformist, and separate. So followers of Jesus are to be discriminating in how we become involved in society. As the Christendom era comes to an end and we rediscover our biblical status as "resident aliens,"[22] maybe the Anabaptist tradition can help us discern when principled withdrawal is more appropriate than collusion, how to assess the benefits and drawbacks of participation, and whether there might sometimes be less conventional ways of being involved.

But aren't Anabaptists all pacifists?

The short answer to this question is simply no. Not all Anabaptists in the sixteenth century were pacifists. Not all Anabaptists in later generations have been pacifists. And not all Anabaptists today are pacifists. This is not a requirement for learning from the tradition or even for participating in many Anabaptist churches and communities.

But the Anabaptist tradition is a peace tradition, and pacifism or nonviolence has been one of its distinguishing features. Unlike their Catholic and Protestant contemporaries, Anabaptists never (with the exception of the Münster aberration) persecuted those with whom they disagreed or attempted to coerce conversion. Pacifism very quickly became the settled conviction of the Anabaptist movement, and it has remained so through the centuries. Some individuals have dissented and some congregations have allowed dissenters to remain, but Anabaptists have continued to advocate nonviolence as the Christian way and, with the Quakers and the Church of the Brethren, comprise what are known as the "historic peace churches."

This commitment to peace is one of the gifts the Anabaptist tradition brings to the wider church. It represents a recovery of the practice of the early churches, a natural expression of what it means to be followers of Jesus in post-Christendom culture where the church is no longer compromised by its partnership with wealth, power, status, and control.[23]

So, if you are not put off by these charges against the Anabaptist tradition, read on.

The Essence of Anabaptism

WHAT, THEN, is the essence of Anabaptism? You might have stumbled across Anabaptists involved in conflict resolution, church planting, peace activism, or campaigning for social justice. You might have encountered Anabaptists in theological tomes or cookbooks. You might, or might not, have associated Anabaptists with traditional communities like the Amish or Hutterites, or dismissed them on the basis of the frequently repeated accusations we considered in the previous chapter. But what do Anabaptists today actually believe? What energizes contemporary Anabaptists and inspires Christians from other traditions when they come across Anabaptism? What does Anabaptism look like when it is stripped down to the bare essentials?

Of course, there is strictly no such thing as a "naked Anabaptist." Anabaptist values and practices are always clothed in particular cultures. Anabaptism was first expressed in the various cultures of the sixteenth-century Swiss, German, and Dutch communities in which it originated. Anabaptist values were embodied differently in the Mennonite, Amish, and Hutterite cultures of subsequent generations in Europe and later in North America.

These values are worked out in fresh ways in parts of the world where Mennonite missionaries have shared their faith and planted churches (while this book was being completed, six thousand representatives from more than fifty nations were meeting in Paraguay for the Mennonite World Conference, a colorful and multicultural gathering of Anabaptists in different clothes). And Anabaptism looks different again in post-Christendom societies in which Christians today are reappropriating its values and practices.

But it is legitimate, and often helpful, to strip back the historical and cultural accretions from traditions that have persisted through the centuries in order to look afresh at what originally inspired them and what continues to attract others to them. It is in this sense that we are investigating in this chapter the essence of Anabaptism and using the image of the "naked Anabaptist" throughout this book.[1]

ANABAPTIST CORE CONVICTIONS

Some years ago, members of the Anabaptist Network in Britain and Ireland put together seven core convictions—our attempt to distill the essence of Anabaptism. Each expresses something we believe and then spells out the commitment to which this belief leads. In the next four chapters, we will explore these convictions in detail as a way of introducing the Anabaptist tradition. We hope that many readers will find these core convictions as inspirational and challenging as we do.[2] Before that, however, please note four disclaimers.

First, these convictions are an attempt by Anabaptists in Britain and Ireland today to learn from the Anabaptist tradition and apply its insights to contemporary issues. They are not an updated version of historic Anabaptist statements, and they deal with some issues that previous generations did not explore.

Second, the Anabaptist Network is a diffuse and diverse community, with no membership criteria. We do not ask those who join to subscribe to our core convictions. Those who join presumably endorse at least some of them, but they are not an ideological filter. The core convictions express the priorities, concerns, and commitments of those who founded the Network and those who have helped shape it over recent years.[3]

Third, these are convictions, not a creed. Anabaptists have generally been wary of fixed statements of faith, which imply there is no need to listen to others or to continue to wrestle with Scripture. Creeds are concerned only with beliefs, but Anabaptists are equally interested in *behavior*. And creeds have often been used to silence, exclude, and persecute dissenters, rather than inviting ongoing conversation. But Anabaptists have produced confessions—statements that are not intended to be comprehensive but set out distinctive convictions and practices. These are always provisional, open to review in light of fresh insights.[4]

Fourth, the commitments spelled out in these core convictions are aspirations rather than achievements. As the first conviction indicates, Anabaptists interpret discipleship as "following" and are very reluctant to claim that they have "arrived." But beliefs do need to have a "so what?" attached.

Bearing in mind these disclaimers, here are the seven core convictions that spell out what it means for many Anabaptists today to identify with this tradition:

1. Jesus is our example, teacher, friend, redeemer, and Lord. He is the source of our life, the central reference point for our faith and lifestyle, for our understanding of church, and our engagement with society. We are committed to following Jesus as well as worshipping him.

2. Jesus is the focal point of God's revelation. We are committed to a Jesus-centered approach to the Bible, and to the community of faith as the primary context in which we read the Bible and discern and apply its implications for discipleship.

3. Western culture is slowly emerging from the Christendom era, when church and state jointly presided over a society in which almost all were assumed to be Christian. Whatever its positive contributions on values and institutions, Christendom seriously distorted the gospel, marginalized Jesus, and has left the churches ill equipped for mission in a post-Christendom culture. As we reflect on this, we are committed to learning from the experience and perspectives of movements such as Anabaptism that rejected standard Christendom assumptions and pursued alternative ways of thinking and behaving.

4. The frequent association of the church with status, wealth, and force is inappropriate for followers of Jesus and damages our witness. We are committed to exploring ways of being

good news to the poor, powerless, and persecuted, aware that such discipleship may attract opposition, resulting in suffering and sometimes ultimately martyrdom.

5. Churches are called to be committed communities of discipleship and mission, places of friendship, mutual accountability, and multivoiced worship. As we eat together, sharing bread and wine, we sustain hope as we seek God's kingdom together. We are committed to nurturing and developing such churches, in which young and old are valued, leadership is consultative, roles are related to gifts rather than gender, and baptism is for believers.

6. Spirituality and economics are interconnected. In an individualist and consumerist culture and in a world where economic injustice is rife, we are committed to finding ways of living simply, sharing generously, caring for creation, and working for justice.

7. Peace is at the heart of the gospel. As followers of Jesus in a divided and violent world, we are committed to finding nonviolent alternatives and to learning how to make peace between individuals, within and among churches, in society, and between nations.

It will be immediately obvious that these statements say nothing at all about foundational theological subjects such as the Trinity, atonement, or eschatology. Nor do they pretend to cover every aspect of subjects they do address, such as Scripture, the church, and mission. These core convictions are not intended to be comprehensive, to substitute for creeds or statements of faith, or to undermine them. Most Anabaptists, today as in the past, gladly affirm the ecumenical creeds that centuries ago established the boundaries of orthodoxy and summarized the essence of the Christian faith—although, as we will see, some point out surprising and worrying omissions from these creeds.

Many Anabaptists also endorse the statements of faith of particular denominations or organizations—although others find these unduly restrictive. The core convictions are supplementary to such creeds or statements of faith. They do not attempt to include everything that Anabaptists share with Christians from other traditions.

Nor do they summarize everything Anabaptists believe. Instead, they concentrate on issues where the Anabaptist tradition has distinctive perspectives.

These perspectives are distinctive rather than unique. Christians from many traditions would affirm at least some of these convictions, even if they would dissent from others or need further clarification of what some of them mean. So perhaps it is the combination of these seven convictions that is representative of the Anabaptist tradition. That is certainly what some who are new to Anabaptism have reported (often with great excitement): these convictions introduce a way of being followers of Jesus that is unusually holistic.

THE IMPACT OF THE CONVICTIONS

The previous chapter featured brief testimonies from various British and Irish Christians who have encountered Anabaptism in recent years. Some of these, and others, have referred to the core convictions as important in their engagement with the Anabaptist tradition. Here is a selection of their comments on these convictions:

Some of the most inspiring people I have met have been Anabaptist in their understanding and following of Jesus Christ. The first two of the core convictions I find inspiring. I thank God for those disciples of Jesus who seek no personal power, fame, or ambition, but only long to be faithful to the kingdom—witnesses to Jesus.
—Brian Haymes (Cheshire, England; on the first and second core convictions)

I found this a very helpful conviction, as it changed the way I viewed the Bible and how I read it. There have been many examples where I have weighed the teaching in the Bible with the character and example of Christ, and it has helped inform my ideas. It is great to be involved with a tradition that values the life of Christ as well as his death and resurrection.
—Sarah Warburton (London; on the second core conviction)

These convictions are related. Christendom and church-growth models have encouraged churches to rely on outside "experts" to do their thinking. The second conviction returns responsibility to the community of faith for their own evangelism and spiritual growth. It is this responsibility which both inspires and challenges.

—*David Kirkman (Annan, Scotland; on the second and third core convictions)*

Christians who recognize the impact of Christendom on the Christian community don't always recognize the extent of the debt in the wider world to Christendom assumptions. The explosive expansion of welcome in the fourth century through the establishment of monasteries, hospices, and hospitals, although in many ways a positive process, also led to the disassociation of the practice of hospitality and its roots in congregations and Christian households. Although a great deal has been accomplished under the Christendom "public service" ethos, many of the essential checks and balances and much of the spirit of "homefulness" inherent in the original congregational crucible of hospitality have been lost. For nearly thirty years, I have sought to bring together my involvement in the housing and homelessness field with Anabaptist commitments to work toward a recovery of the tradition of welcome in a post-Christendom setting.

—*Phil Wood (Wallingford, England; on the third core conviction)*

When we tried to buy an Anglican primary school building for an Anglican church-linked Christian community in the 1970s, but were told it needed to be sold to the highest bidder, we realized that not all churches understood the heart of the gospel as we did. Thirty years later, this Anabaptist conviction energizes our church in supporting asylum seekers and those refused, in coach trips to Scarborough, and in refusing to increase security around the building.

—*Ali Phelps (Leeds, England; on the fourth core conviction)*

The emphasis on community, eating, sharing together, and valuing each other as a base for mission represents for me the essence of church. Relationships, not meetings or structure, should be the basic building blocks of church, and it is so encouraging to find historical examples to help resource the adventure of being church.

—*Linda Wilson (Bristol, England; on the fifth core conviction)*

Long admiring those prisoners of war or conscience, whose faith remains a glowing coal when removed from the fire of the church, I know my need of

close Christian community. To feel both at peace and at home among hospitable people, where all are welcomed, food and friendship as well prayer and multi-voiced worship are shared, is vital to my life.
—Andrew Francis (Swindon, England; on the fifth core conviction)

I'd already been influenced by Anabaptist thinking when I was applying to university in the 1970s. Two of the courses I went for were joint honors: theology and economics; but as the university I went to didn't offer that, I did straight theology, followed by another theology degree at another university. But I balanced that out with a postgraduate degree in finance some years later. After all, Jesus said you can't serve God and money; he didn't say you can't study them both!
—David Nussbaum (Little Chalfont, England; on the sixth core conviction)

It was thanks to my encounter with Anabaptism, where peace is at the heart of things, that I ended up in Northern Ireland. I hoped to practice what I had learned, that peace is "the grain of the universe" and so always possible in the most difficult and violent situations. That is where Jesus is and where the church should be.
—Tim Foley (Portadown, Northern Ireland; on the seventh core conviction)

Nigel Wright (of London, quoting all seven core convictions in a recent book[5]) notes with appreciation their focus on "the centrality of Christ, the primacy of the congregation, and the motif of following after Christ" and concludes that "these deserve to be well known and appreciated in Baptist congregations" (the constituency for which he was writing).

Perhaps these core convictions deserve to be well known and appreciated in other circles too. There may well be some aspects of these convictions, as we explore them in the next four chapters, which will raise questions or cause some readers to balk or take offense. But a growing number of Christians from many traditions have recognized in them a way of understanding the Christian faith that is faithful to the life and teachings of Jesus and that makes sense in a post-Christendom culture.

3

Following Jesus
(Core 1 + 2)

CONTRIBUTING to the Traditions of Christian Spirituality series, Anabaptist historian C. Arnold Snyder entitled his volume on Anabaptist spirituality *Following in the Footsteps of Christ*.[1] The Anabaptist tradition is profoundly Jesus-centered and resonates strongly with the call to "follow" Jesus. The first two core convictions are an attempt by Anabaptists in Britain and Ireland today to spell out some of the implications of following Jesus. This is our starting point.

> Jesus is our example, teacher, friend, redeemer, and Lord. He is the source of our life, the central reference point for our faith and lifestyle, for our understanding of church, and our engagement with society. We are committed to following Jesus as well as worshipping him.

When Anabaptists talk about following Jesus or being Jesus-centered (*Christocentric* if you prefer a theological term), other Christians may be nonplussed or offended. Surely, they respond, all Christians are Jesus-centered and committed to following Jesus. Would that it were that simple! Anabaptists are certainly not claiming that we alone are Jesus-centered or that we are better followers of Jesus than others. In fact, Anabaptists tend to be very reticent about making any claim to spiritual status or achievement. And we recognize in many other traditions wonderful Christians whose lives are centered on Jesus and who are following him faithfully and courageously. But we believe that Jesus has often been marginalized—in practice, if not in theory—in the history of the church and that this legacy is problematic.

FROM THE CENTER TO THE MARGINS

Anabaptists identify the "Christendom shift" in the fourth century as the time when Jesus began to be marginalized. This was when the Roman emperor, Constantine I, adopted the Christian faith and decided to replace paganism with Christianity as the imperial religion. He invited the church to come in from the margins of society, where it had been operating for the previous three centuries, and join him in Christianizing the empire. Lavishing resources and favors on the Christian community, he set in motion a process that would take centuries to complete but would eventually bring all Europe into a sacral society known as "Christendom." In this society the church was no longer on the margins but at the very center, a major landowner, in partnership with the state, and the custodian of moral and spiritual values.

Anabaptists are convinced that, whatever its undoubted benefits, the Christendom system seriously distorted Christian faith. In particular, we believe that the price the church paid for coming in from the margins to the center was allowing Jesus to be pushed out from the center to the margins.

There is plenty of evidence for this. Contrast the sermons preached at the end of the third century with those preached at the end of the fourth, and ask where the teaching of Jesus has gone. Compare pre-Christendom artwork with Christendom depictions of Jesus and note how the good shepherd has been replaced by a remote, imperial figure (not unlike Constantine, in fact). Consider the ecumenical creeds produced in the early Christendom period, which move straight from Jesus' birth to his death ("born of the Virgin Mary, suffered under Pontius Pilate"), with no reference to his life.

Some earlier creeds may not have included much more about the life of Jesus, but they were accompanied by careful formation of new Christians (known as "catechesis"), in which the life and teachings of Jesus figured strongly. By the end of the fourth century, the catechesis system was being overwhelmed by the numbers flooding into the churches now that Christianity enjoyed imperial favor. Much less time was now devoted to the teaching of Jesus. The emphasis was on uniformity of belief and avoiding heresy, rather than counter-cultural discipleship. The creeds were crucially important to this process, but it seems the life and teachings of Jesus were not.

There were understandable reasons why the imperial church marginalized Jesus as fourth-century Christians struggled to adapt to a new social and political context. His teaching, which had been challenging enough for a powerless, marginal community, seemed utterly unrealistic and inapplicable for Christians assuming responsibility for an empire. What now did it mean to "love your enemies" (Matthew 5:44) or "do not worry about tomorrow" (6:34)? How could such instructions be translated into foreign or economic policies? Jesus seemed not to have anticipated this development or to have given any counsel to those with an imperial administration to run. Gratefully, church leaders turned instead to the Old Testament for guidance: after all, ancient Israel had an economy to run, borders to defend, and a social system to organize.

Nor were the teachings of Jesus the only problem. More awkward still was his lifestyle, his passion for justice, his confrontations with the wealthy and powerful (the very people whom the churches were now wooing), his care for the outcasts and the downtrodden, his refusal to endorse social norms and traditional gender roles. As the church mixed ever more with the "movers and shakers," it was difficult to know what it meant to follow and imitate the "friend of sinners" who prioritized the "moved and shaken." As the churches accepted and relished an honored place in a hierarchical society, the upside-down, last-will-be-first values Jesus taught and practiced were disturbing and distasteful.

Even worse was the embarrassing memory that Jesus had been killed by the same Roman Empire that now wanted him as its figurehead. There was no getting away from this, even though many tried to pin the blame on the Jews as the "Christ killers." To their credit, those who framed the creeds named the Roman governor Pontius Pilate as responsible for the execution of Jesus. The cross symbolized powerfully to the early Christians the triumph of love over hatred, forgiveness over vengeance, the laying down of life rather than the taking of life. But it also represented the brutality and oppression of the Roman Empire that threatened to destroy them as it had attempted to silence Jesus. Now that the persecution had ended, this memory must be suppressed and this potent symbol must be reinterpreted.

What could the imperial church do? Obviously, their founder could not be airbrushed out of the story altogether. But the life and teaching of Jesus could be reappraised, neutered, and domesticated. The way in which the Sermon on the Mount was handled during the Christendom era is a classic example of this process. Theologians and preachers found several ingenious ways of evading its challenge. Some insisted it was mandatory for the clergy and the monks but beyond the reach of most Christians. Others said it did not refer to the present age but described life in the coming kingdom of God. Many suggested it applied only to the private sphere, not to public life in the empire. Another interpretation offered reassurance that it was not meant to be obeyed but to show the impossibility of obedience and so throw you back on the grace of God. Or perhaps it applied only to interior attitudes, not to outward behavior, so that it was possible to love the enemies into whom you were thrusting your sword.

WORSHIPPED BUT NOT FOLLOWED
These strategies ensured that the teaching of Jesus could be simultaneously honored and ignored. In the same way, by recasting him as a remote, imperial figure and emphasizing his divinity much more than his humanity, the imperial church could worship and honor Jesus without needing to listen to him, imitate his example, or follow him. Jesus could be effectively marginalized without apparently being dishonored.

But it was the startling reinterpretation of the meaning of the cross that represented the greatest triumph (or compromise) of imperial Christianity. No longer a symbol of nonviolent sacrificial love, the cross was brazenly converted into a military standard. Armies marched to battle under the sign of the cross and "taking up the cross" meant readiness to kill rather than to die.[2]

Throughout the Christendom era, Anabaptists claim, Jesus was marginalized in these and other ways. There were various reactions to this marginalization. The monastic movement was an attempt to return to the radical teachings of Jesus and live by them. Christian mystics and renewal movements rejected the remoteness of Christ, sought intimacy with Jesus, and advocated the imitation of

Christ. And the sixteenth-century Anabaptists were the latest in a long line of dissident movements inspired and shaped by reading the Gospels, rediscovering Jesus, and determining to follow him.

But the mainstream churches—Catholic and Protestant—continued to marginalize Jesus. He was worshipped rather than followed. The Protestant reformers honored Jesus as the one through whose redeeming work sinful human beings could be justified, but they generally paid scant attention to his life and teaching. They read Paul's letters avidly but were not particularly interested in the Gospels. Martin Luther wrote, "If we had to do without one or the other, it would be better to lack the works and the history than the words and the doctrine."[3] The reformers agreed with Anabaptists that Jesus was "the source of our life," but it seems clear that it was the death of Jesus, rather than Jesus himself, who was at the center of their faith. It is clear from their writings that he was not "the central reference point for our faith and lifestyle, for our understanding of church, and our engagement with society."

Sixteenth-century Anabaptists embraced a passionately Jesus-centered approach that impacted every aspect of discipleship. They challenged the Christendom tradition, which had found the radical Jesus hard to cope with in a world Christians now controlled. They critiqued popular expressions of medieval piety that spiritualized and privatized devotion to Jesus. And they provoked the reformers, who thundered the centrality of Jesus for salvation but seemed reticent about allowing Jesus' life and teaching to be normative for lifestyle, church, and mission. For the Anabaptists, being Jesus-centered was a choice of ultimate loyalties, but the reformers seemed reluctant to risk the wrath of the political authorities by applying his teaching to social and economic issues.

This is the background to our first core conviction. We believe that the Christendom era has bequeathed a form of Christianity that has marginalized, spiritualized, domesticated, and emasculated Jesus. The teaching of Jesus is watered down, privatized, and explained away. Jesus is worshipped as a remote kingly figure or a romanticized personal savior. In many churches (especially those emerging from the Reformation), Paul's writings are prioritized over the Gospel accounts of the life of Jesus. And in many Christian traditions, ethical guidelines derived from the Old Testament or pagan philosophy trump Jesus' call to discipleship.

FROM THE MARGINS TO THE CENTER?

But as the Christendom era draws to a close and the churches find themselves back on the margins, no longer feted or favored by society, there are signs that Jesus might be making something of a comeback. Here's a sample of the evidence:

For over a century, biblical scholars have been on a "quest for the historical Jesus" (actually several quests), attempting to peel back layers of tradition and encounter Jesus afresh. The wildly divergent accounts of Jesus emerging from this research have frequently been criticized for merely endorsing the researchers' assumptions and prejudices—but at least the life of Jesus is the source of debate once more.

The popular but oft-derided WWJD ("what would Jesus do?") bracelets worn by thousands of enthusiastic Christians may provoke similar criticism. Ascribing our ethical decisions to "what Jesus would do" may be an exercise in self-deception. It certainly begs many questions about the basis on which we attempt to answer this question. But at least Jesus is acknowledged as "the central reference point for our faith and lifestyle."

Anabaptist writers, and others, have rejected the domestication of Jesus' teaching. They have demonstrated how it applies to political, social, and economic issues and that it is much more radical than Christendom's commentators allowed. The impact of John Howard Yoder's *The Politics of Jesus* was profound, introducing Christians from many traditions to a new way of reading the Gospels. *The Upside-Down Kingdom* by Donald Kraybill gently but devastatingly dismantled centuries of misinterpretation of the Sermon on the Mount. Marcus Borg, Brian McLaren, Walter Wink, Shane Claiborne, Tom Wright, Steve Chalke, Michael Frost, and Alan Hirsch are just a few of those—some more influenced by Anabaptism than others—who (in scholarly or popular books) have redirected our attention to the life of Jesus and encouraged us to take a fresh look at what he taught.[4]

Research into emerging churches in Europe and North America reveals renewed interest in the Gospels and the life and teaching of Jesus. Eddie Gibbs and Ryan Bolger identified nine core practices of the emerging churches they surveyed, the first of which was "identifying with the life of Jesus."[5] And John Drane concludes, "Jesus is central for the emerging church, not so much as an object of belief but as an example to be followed." It is the Jesus of the Gospels, he argues, rather than the Jesus of the creeds, who inspires and challenges many Christians today.[6]

In post-Christendom societies, most people are unfamiliar with theological terms, biblically illiterate, and disparaging of the church as an institution. But many still claim to be Christians, and Jesus is respected and often intriguing—however little is known of his life and teachings. Filmmakers continue to find ready audiences for portrayals of the life of Jesus—some of these arguably (and despite often ill-conceived protests from the Christian community) more authentic than portrayals in sermons and Sunday school talks.

So there is renewed interest in the life and teaching of Jesus among Christians, and there is continuing respect for Jesus (if not the churches) in post-Christendom societies. Maybe together we can all rediscover the Jesus who was marginalized during the Christendom era. Such a rediscovery might be a potent resource for our witness as we participate in God's mission today. It might also transform our lives and our churches.

What does the Anabaptist tradition offer toward this rediscovery? Perhaps the most helpful resource is five hundred years of practice and reflection on what it means to regard Jesus as "example," "teacher," and "the central reference point for our faith and lifestyle." The Anabaptist story contains warnings as well as encouragements. Instances of failure and compromise jostle with examples of faithfulness and consistency. But, rejecting the Christendom system earlier than most and determining that the life and teaching of Jesus would be central to their faith, Anabaptists have had a long time to explore the implications of "following Jesus as well as worshipping him."

FOLLOWING JESUS

"Following Jesus" is a central motif in the Anabaptist tradition. One of the most widely quoted sixteenth-century Anabaptist statements is Hans Denck's assertion "No one can know Christ unless he follows after him in life."[7] All claims to spiritual experience or doctrinal orthodoxy were to be tested against practical discipleship. Anabaptists were charged with reverting to "salvation by works," but they replied that their critics were well aware of the abysmally low standards of discipleship in their own churches and should ask why their supposedly correct doctrine was producing so little fruit.

Critics were irritated by this response but were unsure how to counter it. The Anabaptists might be heretics, but their lifestyle was undoubtedly distinctive and attractive. Franz Agricola, a sixteenth-century Roman Catholic opponent, expressed his confusion:

> As concerns their outward public life they are irreproachable. No lying, deception, swearing, strife, harsh language, no intemperate eating and drinking, no outward personal display, is found among them, but humility, patience, uprightness, neatness, honesty, temperance, straightforwardness in such measure that one would suppose that they had the Holy Spirit of God![8]

There are even accounts of non-Anabaptists arrested on suspicion of being Anabaptists because they lived good lives—and escaping prosecution only by cursing freely and persuading their accusers that they were not really as holy as they appeared.

In fact, Agricola's explanation—"that they had the Holy Spirit of God"—was the reason Anabaptists themselves offered for the way they lived. Agricola dismissed this because heretics could not have the Holy Spirit in this way, but Anabaptists placed a much greater emphasis than their contemporaries on the work of the Holy Spirit, bringing about their "new birth" and their experience of the transformative power of God's grace. Lives of faithful discipleship were not a result of striving to earn their salvation, nor a cause for pride, but evidence that God was truly at work in them.

The rest of Denck's saying is less well known but points to another aspect of this core conviction: for Anabaptists Jesus is the source of our life as well as the one we follow. Denck insisted, "No one can follow him unless he first know him." Following Christ is inseparably related to knowing Christ.

Anabaptists today, then, find both inspiration and challenge in this tradition. Jesus can be followed faithfully. His example can instruct us. His teaching can be practiced. Worship and discipleship can be integrated. Jesus can be the central reference point for all of life. And these convictions need not degenerate into legalism or moralism if we recognize him as the source of our life and as our friend as well as our Lord.

Ali Phelps, a member of the Anabaptist Network steering group and one of the leaders of an inner-city Baptist church in Leeds, read a draft of this chapter and wrote to me:

> Following Jesus reminded me of our response to a belligerent challenge by a confronting lesbian to our (mainly conservative) congregation. I agreed to read the Gospel of Luke with her—mostly out of cowardice on my part, preferring to hide behind the person of Jesus than debate church theory or practice. She became a passionate follower long before we'd completed our task. Some time later she stunned me by announcing she'd given up cannabis. When I asked who had been questioning her behavior, she said that it was a direct and obvious response to scripture and that if anyone in the congregation had challenged her, she would have reacted badly and redoubled her consumption!

This aspect of the Anabaptist tradition might also have missional significance in a context where the story of Jesus is relatively unknown but where the human figure of Jesus is still accorded respect. In post-Christendom, evangelism will need to begin with story-telling if we are to start where most people are, and telling the story—and the stories—of Jesus of Nazareth may be more potent than we realize. An Anglican priest recently reported that he had used the parable of the prodigal son in pastoral ministry toward someone with no church connections. She had not only found it helpful and moving but asked, "Who told that story?" and, when informed that it was Jesus, enquired, "Did he tell any other stories?" We might just find that evangelism is much simpler than we think—telling the story of Jesus and letting him speak for himself.

The motif of "following Jesus" may also help us find a path through the confusion around "belonging," "believing," and "behaving" that many churches are experiencing. "Belonging before believing" may accurately describe how many people engage with our churches. It may be the approach to mission we advocate in a postmodern, post-Christendom culture. But there are complexities and challenges underneath this catchy slogan:

- How does belonging evolve into believing, and how often does this happen?
- How many people can belong before they believe without the church losing coherence?
- How does behaving relate to belonging and believing?
- What does belonging actually mean without believing and behaving?
- Why are believing and behaving often disconnected?

The language of "following" offers an integrating framework for churches who want to be welcoming and inclusive but also want to see movement toward believing and behaving.

In the Gospels, crowds followed Jesus, and he welcomed all who came to him, regardless of their lifestyle, teaching and healing indiscriminately on most occasions, sharing meals with disreputable people and with those who were hostile to his teaching. But Jesus also called those who were hanging out with him to change their behavior and rethink their beliefs. Among the crowds were his disciples— those who had responded decisively to the call to follow, even if they continued to struggle with the implications of this—and others who from time to time responded by behaving in new ways (for example, Zacchaeus; see Luke 19:1-10) or believing in Jesus (for example, the centurion whose servant Jesus healed; see 7:1-10). Sometimes Jesus' teaching seems to be directed primarily at the disciples, with everyone else listening in; sometimes Jesus is teaching the crowds, but the disciples are also learning from him.

Maybe we need to stop calling ourselves "Christians." Not only is this term compromised by its associations and debased by overuse, it is also rather presumptuous. Who are we to claim that we are like Christ? If others want to refer to us in this way, because they see us as Christlike, well and good—this seems to have been how the term was first used (see Acts 11:26). But maybe we need a term that is both purposeful and restrained. Maybe we should claim no more (or less) than that we are "followers of Jesus."

As followers, we do not claim to have arrived at the destination, nor need we distinguish ourselves from others who are at different stages of the journey. Belonging, believing, and behaving can all be interpreted as aspects of following. Churches committed to following Jesus welcome fellow travelers unreservedly and unconditionally. But their ethos is one of following, learning, changing, growing, moving forward. Together, and as we reflect on the Gospels (and the rest of Scripture), we discover more of what it means to follow Jesus.

Such churches may be very good news indeed to those who need time to work through the implications of the story of Jesus that they have encountered for the first time. And to those who are more interested in lifestyle issues than theological beliefs. And to those who use "journey" imagery to describe their search for spiritual meaning. And to those of us who know we still have some way to go in following Jesus and are grateful for the support and encouragement of others who are on the same journey.

So should followers of Jesus ask, "What would Jesus do?" There are many worse questions to ask when faced with ethical dilemmas. But Anabaptists will be wary, not only that we may be overconfident that we know the answer, but that the Jesus to whom we refer may be the domesticated, co-opted, or emasculated Jesus of Christendom.

Other questions may be more helpful: What *did* Jesus do? What did Jesus *say*? What was Jesus *like*? Engaging with these questions takes us back to the Gospels and encourages us to listen carefully to Jesus and to learn from his example. This was what the early Anabaptists insisted on doing, to the discomfort of their critics, who preferred to rely on general principles (such as love, justice, and order) rather than the specifics of the life and teaching of Jesus. But if Jesus is truly to be our "central reference point," we need to start with what he actually said and did.

Which leads conveniently into our second core conviction:

> Jesus is the focal point of God's revelation. We are committed to a Jesus-centered approach to the Bible and to the community of faith as the primary context in which we read the Bible and discern and apply its implications for discipleship.

The Anabaptist movement began at a time when the Bible was newly available to people. Translations into German and other European languages coincided with the arrival of the printing press. After centuries when only the clergy and monks had access to the Bible or the ability to read it in Latin or its original languages, Bibles in languages everyone could understand were disseminated across Europe. Literacy was severely limited, and Bibles were hugely expensive (affordable only by wealthy individuals or communities pooling their resources). But wherever Bibles could be obtained and someone was available who could read the text aloud, small groups gathered to listen and to reflect together on what they heard. The Anabaptists were not the only ones studying and discussing the Bible in the early sixteenth century.

And, shockingly, the reformers seemed to be encouraging people to interpret the Bible for *themselves*, rather than relying on traditional understandings and the pronouncements of popes and church councils. "Scripture alone!" they insisted, confident that anyone with access to the text of Scripture would share their convictions about what it meant. Much to their surprise and discomfort, not everyone did. In fact, many questioned the interpretations of the reformers as well as the Catholic hierarchy, and some began to apply the Bible to social, political, and economic realities in very disturbing ways. Many features of church and society, they suggested, seemed to have little biblical support. Indeed, some seemed to be contradicted by biblical teaching. As in previous generations, reading the Bible—and especially the Gospels—without the guidance of authorized interpreters provoked people to challenge traditional assumptions and well-established practices.

Realizing the dangers, the reformers tried to put the cork back in the bottle, insisting that people should abide by the interpretations of their preachers and pastors, but it was too late. Many refused to exchange the old system of a priestly monopoly on what the Bible "must mean" for a new system that gave this monopoly to the preachers. Among these were the early Anabaptists, who were captivated by the Jesus of the Gospels and who were becoming increasingly convinced that the Bible had been misinterpreted on all kinds of topics for a very long time.

Several convictions characterized the way Anabaptists read and interpreted the Bible:

- They were confident that ordinary Christians, who had not received theological training or official accreditation but who were attentive to the Holy Spirit, could interpret the Bible responsibly.

- They believed that the congregation, not the seminary or preacher's study, was the place where the Bible should be interpreted; understanding the Bible was a community practice.

- Their focus was on practical application—discovering what the Bible meant for discipleship, rather than just searching out its original meaning.

- They insisted that the Bible must be interpreted in light of the life, teaching, death, and resurrection of Jesus Christ. Jesus was the center of the Bible, the one to whom both Testaments pointed.

This approach seemed arrogant, irresponsible, and chaotic to their critics. But Anabaptists found it liberating and empowering. And when they read the Bible together in this way, they discovered alternative possibilities on a range of theological, ecclesial, and ethical issues.

It was in the area of ethics that the teachings of Jesus seemed to have been marginalized in favor of Old Testament practices. Making war, executing criminals, swearing oaths, ascribing a divinely granted status to kings, and extracting tithes could all be justified from the Old Testament, but were these practices really congruent with what Jesus said and did? The reformers appeared to Anabaptists to have a flat Bible, picking out principles from anywhere without reference to the unfolding purposes of God. The Anabaptists rejected this approach and insisted that the Bible needed to be interpreted in light of the teachings and example of Jesus. But those who were determined to maintain the Christendom system could not tolerate this.[9]

Anabaptists today, with the benefit of hindsight, may be more aware of weaknesses in the early Anabaptists' approach to biblical interpretation. Distrusting scholarship deprives us of helpful resources with which to better understand the Bible; scholarship need not, as the early Anabaptists feared, distort or evade the text. Trusting the Holy Spirit to enable interpreters does not mean that the text becomes straightforward and free of difficulties. Protesting against the misuse of the Old Testament to justify practices that are hard to square with the life and teachings of Jesus need not mean that we marginalize the Old Testament. And locating the task of biblical interpretation in the local congregation not only risks ignoring the wisdom of previous generations but can set congregation against congregation.

Nevertheless, many of us continue to be grateful for the courage and imagination of the early Anabaptists as they pioneered a new approach to biblical interpretation.[10] We also find it interesting that many of the conclusions to which their supposedly unsophisticated and illegitimate approach led them are now widely accepted by Christians in many other traditions. Our second core conviction focuses on three foundational aspects of the way in which they engaged with Scripture.

IMPLICATIONS FOR DISCIPLESHIP

An emphasis on Christian discipleship has been one of the attractions and challenges of the Anabaptist tradition. All the core convictions we are examining involve a call to serious discipleship in different areas of life. These are undergirded by an approach to the Bible that refuses to separate interpretation from application.

While we may not share the distrust of the early Anabaptists toward biblical scholars—whom they accused of relying on human reason rather than spiritual insight, evading the plain meaning of the text because of the cost of obeying it, wasting time on questions that were of interest only to other scholars, and allowing vested interests to determine their conclusions—we may have some sympathy with their concerns. Many perceive a gulf between the academy and the congregation. Biblical scholars are usually unaccountable and in no position to test out the implications of their interpretations of Scripture. Bible studies in the local congregation often represent an unedifying pooling of ignorance and rarely move beyond searching for the meaning of the text to exploring its implications for discipleship—let alone developing processes that hold one another accountable to follow through in practice what has been discerned.

This second core conviction commits us to integrate interpretation and application. Bible study that does not lead to more faithful and creative discipleship is inadequate. There are some similarities between this conviction and the approach of Latin American liberation theologians,[11] who insist that the goal of interpretation is not to understand the Bible but to discover from the Bible how to live faithfully. They advocate a process of action and reflection in which application feeds back into deeper reflection on the text, and the text stimulates renewed action. Early Anabaptists were convinced that interpreters would not make progress in understanding the Bible unless they were already practicing what they did understand. And as they attempted to put into practice what they believed Scripture taught, the consequences would help them discern whether they had understood the text well.

Anabaptists today may be more aware of the influence of the interpreter's background and presuppositions, although early Anabaptists claimed that being on the margins of society and subject to persecution gave them significant advantages in understanding the New Testament, which was written to people in similar circumstances. We bring who we are, our interests and perspectives, to the task of biblical interpretation. We cannot escape this influence, although recognizing it can mitigate its impact, as can reading the Bible with Christians from other cultures who bring different assumptions and questions. But we will be wary of allowing the increasingly diverse and sophisticated approaches to biblical interpretation emanating from the academy to distract us from the challenge of applying biblical teaching in ways that foster faithful discipleship.

THE COMMUNITY OF FAITH

We will also resist approaches to biblical interpretation that disempower the Christian community. While the early Anabaptists endorsed the freedom and responsibility of all believers to read (or hear) the Bible and interpret it with the help of the Holy Spirit, they expected this process to take place primarily within the congregation. In fact, it was when those in the community of faith gathered and reflected on Scripture together that they anticipated the Spirit would guide them and bring them to one mind about what the text meant and how they were to apply it. Individualistic interpretations that were not open to weighing by the congregation were considered illegitimate and dangerous.

It was not only the emphasis on discipleship that was stronger among the Anabaptists than among most of their contemporaries. So too was their commitment to community and their expectation that all members of the community would be active and vocal participants, rather than passive spectators. This was one of their criticisms of the state churches, Catholic and Protestant, and a reason many gave for not attending those churches.[12] They could not understand why everyone deferred to the preacher and did not contribute to the task of biblical interpretation. Surely Paul had made it clear in 1 Corinthians 14 that many gifts were needed and many voices should be heard and that all contributions were to be tested, not just accepted without question.

The role of the community of faith was, and still is, diminished by excessive reliance on expert interpreters, unaccountable individual interpretations, and unwarranted deference to those who preach and teach. Scholars, preachers, and inspired individuals may all help us interpret and apply the Bible, but the community of faith is the primary context where what each brings can be weighed. It is also the primary context in which we can weigh the results of applying what we understand the Bible to teach and reflect further on what we have learned as we have tried to practice our faith.

Some Anabaptists today are encouraging congregations to take up this challenge, aware that it will require the retraining of preachers and communities, and very considerable perseverance, if mono-voiced churches are to evolve into multivoiced churches. Founder members of the Anabaptist Network Alan and Eleanor Kreider are well known to many for their distinctive "speaking together" style as they model an alternative to mono-voiced preaching. For many years I have practiced interactive preaching, inviting congregations to engage with what I am saying, rather than simply to listen to me preach. Another member of the Network, Graham Old, has set up an "interactive preaching" website to encourage the development of this practice and to share ideas and resources.[13]

I also discovered, during a visit to Pennsylvania in 2009, a group of Mennonite churches using a practice they called "dwelling in the word." This resembles *lectio divina*, a monastic practice that is becoming increasingly popular among laypeople, after which participants are invited to share their own responses to Scripture. But "dwelling in the word," which gives congregations an opportunity to reflect together on a passage that will shortly be the basis for a sermon, invites participants to listen carefully to each other and then report to others how someone else has responded to this passage. This practice seemed to me better suited to an Anabaptist community than the more individualistic practice of *lectio divina*.

Responses to these more interactive and participative approaches to biblical interpretation have been mixed. Many preachers recognize the limitations of mono-voiced preaching and are enthusiastic about a multivoiced approach, but they are unsure whether they can adapt and uncertain how their congregations will react. Initial experiences may be discouraging as they learn new skills and as members of their congregations grumble about these innovations. Some give up rather than struggling on. The temptation to revert to the more familiar and less demanding default mono-voiced approach will undoubtedly be very strong. But the level of dissatisfaction with preacher-dominated church life and individualistic discipleship may now be strong enough to enable some communities to resist.

JESUS-CENTERED INTERPRETATION

If some are drawn to Anabaptism today by its emphasis on discipleship or community, many others are drawn by the central place given to the life and teaching of Jesus. We have already explored the Christocentrism of Anabaptism as a movement. This was rooted in and resulted in a determined Christocentrism in biblical interpretation. *Determined* is the appropriate word. Early Anabaptists were scandalized by the way Jesus was being marginalized in systems of biblical interpretation that seemed to privilege other parts of Scripture over what Jesus said and did. They regarded this as dishonoring Jesus and were determined to challenge it.

For Anabaptists, as for the anonymous author of the book of Hebrews and most other Christians, Jesus is the focal point of God's revelation. "Long ago God spoke to our ancestors in many and various ways by the prophets, but in these last days he has spoken to us by a Son, whom he appointed heir of all things, through whom he also created the worlds" (Hebrews 1:1-2). For Anabaptists, but not always for Christians in other traditions, this means that the Bible, as a record of what God has said and done in many generations, must be viewed through the prism of the revelation of God in Jesus Christ. The Old Testament points forward to him; the New Testament points back to him.

Contrary to Luther's preference for doctrinal texts, this means giving particular priority to those parts of the Bible in which the life and teachings of Jesus are most evident, namely the Gospels. It was these narrative accounts, with their provocative encounters and their enigmatic but challenging teaching, culminating in the death and resurrection of the One who was too threatening for the religious and political establishments, that Anabaptists studied with great intensity. It was these texts that Anabaptists treated as the interpretive center of Scripture.

This approach has its critics. Prioritizing any part of Scripture risks downgrading the rest. The life of Jesus makes sense only in light of the history, theology, prophecy, and imagery of the Old Testament. Other parts of the New Testament were not only written before the Gospels but also add significantly to our understanding of Jesus.

Some of those who have been occupied in the "quest for the historical Jesus" pour scorn on any suggestion that we can trust these accounts as a reliable record of what Jesus actually said and did. But Anabaptists today remain convinced that if Jesus really is "the focal point of God's revelation," these accounts of his life, teaching, death, and resurrection must be central to our understanding of the whole of God's revelation in Scripture. Our experience is that a Jesus-centered approach to Scripture results in different ways of interpreting the Bible on issues such as nonviolence, truth telling, economics, power, gender relations, mission, and the nature of the church.

POSTSCRIPT

For many years I have taught a session on the Workshop program entitled "Jesus at the Center," starting with the verses from Hebrews quoted above, explaining how Jesus was marginalized under Christendom, and asking what difference it might make if we were to restore Jesus to his rightful place at the center. The impact of this session has been greater than any other I have taught anywhere on any subject. Many students have told me (some years later, when I next encountered them) that this was when all kinds of lights went on for them. For some it had resulted in life-changing decisions. For others it had galvanized their faith and renewed their vision of what God was calling them into.

Some had expected little from this session. After all, as Christians they already knew that Jesus was at the center—or at least that he was meant to be. But as they started to realize the malign influence of the Christendom shift on this aspect of their faith, many decided to go back to the Gospels, listen afresh to Jesus, and accept the consequences of following as well as worshipping him.

The Anabaptist tradition, with its pungent critique of Christendom and determination to be Jesus-centered, may have been the catalyst (and some began to identify themselves as Anabaptists), but what they did was what Christians in many previous generations have done—return to the Gospels and rediscover the radical Jesus. No Christian tradition has a monopoly on this. Jesus-centered discipleship keeps being rediscovered. But, with all its weaknesses, Anabaptism seems to have an unusual capacity to provoke Christians from many traditions (and some who are not yet Christians) to encounter Jesus afresh.

4

After Christendom

THE THIRD and fourth core convictions spell out why Anabaptists today tend to celebrate rather than grieve the end of Christendom.

We encountered the Christendom system in the previous chapter. We considered there its impact on how Christians have read the Bible and how the church has engaged with the life and teaching of Jesus. But there is more to be said about a system that has dominated Europe for centuries and has been exported across the globe via mission and conquest. Christendom was a remarkable and brilliant culture, but it was also totalitarian and often brutal. It has assumed various shapes at different times and in different parts of the world, but these several versions of Christendom share a common ideology.

Anabaptists and other dissident movements during the Christendom centuries started by objecting to doctrines and practices they believed were unbiblical or unchristian. This prompted them to question a system that allowed or required such beliefs and behavior. Eventually they rejected Christendom as fundamentally flawed, disengaged from it, and formed alternative communities in which they experimented with alternative approaches to discipleship.

Rejecting Christendom brought down on their heads the wrath of church and state. These movements were accused of treason and sedition as well as heresy. They were persecuted for undermining the sacral society that was Christendom. Some were eradicated, and little information survives about what they did and taught: almost all we know of them comes from their (hardly unbiased) opponents. But the Anabaptist movement survived severe persecution and has preserved the wisdom and experience of generations of Christians who pursued alternative ways of thinking and behaving.

As the Christendom system disintegrates, many Christians in western societies today are learning from the Anabaptist tradition how to be followers of Jesus in a world we no longer control or dominate. The legacy of Christendom is mixed. Perhaps the Anabaptists and other dissidents overreacted and failed to appreciate the achievements and treasures of Christendom. But this alternative tradition offers to post-Christendom Christians many resources that the mainstream traditions, wedded to Christendom assumptions, have not realized would be needed.

> Western culture is slowly emerging from the Christendom era when church and state jointly presided over a society in which almost all were assumed to be Christian. Whatever its positive contributions to values and institutions, Christendom seriously distorted the gospel, marginalized Jesus, and has left the churches ill equipped for mission in a post-Christendom culture. As we reflect on this, we are committed to learning from the experience and perspectives of movements such as Anabaptism that rejected standard Christendom assumptions and pursued alternative ways of thinking and behaving.

WHAT WAS CHRISTENDOM?

Post-Christendom is one of many "post" terms commentators are using to describe the shifts taking place in western culture. There are numerous others: postmodern, post-industrial, post-colonial, post-imperial, post-secular, and more. The *post* prefix means "after" and indicates that we are experiencing a time of transition. Familiar features of the social landscape are disappearing into the past, but it is not yet clear what is emerging out of the mist of the future. "Post" language is modest but honest. It tells us that we are no longer where we used to be, but does not pretend to know exactly where we are heading. If we knew what was coming, we could abandon "post" terms and name the emerging reality. But we are not there yet. So we use "post" terms to signal change and uncertainty.

"Post" terms invite us to look back to what was, in order to prepare for what is coming. If we are to grasp the implications of whatever post-Christendom is becoming, we will need first to understand what Christendom was. What were its defining features? What were its strengths and weaknesses? What is its legacy and its continuing influence, for good or ill?

Our third core conviction suggests that the period of transition from Christendom to post-Christendom will not be rapid. Christendom persisted for centuries and has permeated all aspects of western societies. Vestiges of this civilization will remain long after the system itself has crumbled. For many years yet, we will live in the overlap between Christendom and post-Christendom. What will we attempt to preserve from the past and what will we gladly consign to history? What will need to change and what should stay the same? All Christian traditions are grappling with these questions. The Anabaptist tradition does not claim to have all the answers, but it offers distinctive perspectives earthed in almost five centuries of exploring alternatives to Christendom.

What, then, was Christendom?

- Christendom was a geographical region in which almost everyone was at least nominally Christian.

- Christendom was a historical era resulting from the fourth-century conversion of Constantine and lasting into the late twentieth century.

- Christendom was a civilization decisively shaped by the story, language, symbols, and rhythms of Christianity.

- Christendom was a political arrangement in which church and state provided mutual, if often uneasy, support and legitimation.

- Christendom was an ideology, a mindset, a way of thinking about God's activity in the world.

The "Christendom shift" originated in the fourth century. Constantine and his successors (with one brief exception) embraced Christianity, and gradually the pagan Roman Empire became officially Christian. Through a mixture of persuasion, inducements, and force, the empire's citizens adopted this new faith. Other religions were suppressed and paganism was eventually outlawed, although many vestiges remained centuries later, especially in rural areas. Only the Jews remained as a dissident community. The Holy Roman Empire (as it became known) was no more successful in assimilating them than the pagan empire had been, despite much more efficient persecution and persistent efforts to convert them. But pretty much everyone else was now Christian—by birth rather than by choice. The question "Are you a Christian?" had become meaningless in a society where this was the default position.

Christendom spread. Missionaries carried the gospel (and imperial Christian culture) to lands and tribes beyond the old imperial boundaries. Imperial armies, fighting under the "sign of the cross," conquered new territories and imposed the Christian faith on peoples they conquered. By the year 1000, almost all Europeans were members of Christendom. Beyond lay "heathendom," strange cultures and civilizations, into which missionaries and armies made occasional forays. But most Christendom Christians, unlike Christians in the early churches, had no contact at all with other civilizations, faiths, or cultures. Nor were they in touch with the large Christian communities in Asia beyond the boundaries of their world—communities that thrived for centuries without a Christendom support system.[1]

At its height in the Middle Ages, Christendom was a powerful, wealthy, creative, and self-confident civilization. Theology and philosophy flourished. Artists and sculptors, poets and musicians, architects and writers, interpreted, contextualized, and embedded Christian themes and values in their buildings, literature, songs, and statues. Christian theology and ethics provided the framework for legislation and judicial practices. The stages of human life were marked by Christian rituals, and the rhythm of the seasons was punctuated by Christian festivals. The Christian story shaped Christendom culture.

Undergirding this civilization was the notion of a "sacral society," in which religion and politics, public and private, church and state were fully integrated. Christendom did not recognize the sacred/secular divide with which modern western societies are familiar. The two pillars of this civilization were church and state, recognizably different in form and function, but inextricably linked as partners controlling society. Sometimes the emperor dominated the pope; sometimes the pope demanded obedience from the emperor. Power dynamics shifted, but this mutually beneficial partnership persisted. State power backed up the spiritual and moral requirements of the church, which in turn blessed the policies and actions of the state.

This partnership (some would say collusion) between church and state was responsible for other features of Christendom that few now would justify. Whatever the undoubted accomplishments of Christendom, this was a brutal civilization that terrorized its own subjects through inquisition, torture, and witch hunts; oppressed them through a deeply resented tithing system; persecuted dissidents; and expanded its influence through wars, forced baptisms, and crusades. Christendom, as the Anabaptists argued in the sixteenth century (and many now would acknowledge), distorted the gospel it claimed to uphold.

In the fifteenth and sixteenth centuries, Christendom both fragmented and expanded. The discovery of the "New World" presented the opportunity of bringing new territories under the sway of Christendom. Through the familiar combination of conquest and mission, the diverse peoples of the Americas were swept into Christendom and European culture was exported as a crucial part of this process. European culture was, naturally, regarded as Christian and indubitably superior to all others. Forgetting that the Christian faith had been contextualized centuries earlier into European society, Christendom missionaries usually assumed that their cultural expression of Christianity was normative, and they imposed this everywhere. Though there were early exceptions, most missionaries (and missionary societies) only gradually came to realize that Christian faith could be incarnated in many different cultures and that other cultures brought gifts European civilization needed to receive.

But this period of expansion coincided with the fragmentation of Christendom. Despite their best intentions, the sixteenth-century reformers, who were attempting to purify and renew the church, ended up fracturing Christendom into competing mini-Christendoms— Lutheran, Reformed, Calvinist, Catholic, and Anglican. There had, of course, been an earlier painful schism between the (western) Catholic and (eastern) Orthodox branches of Christendom, but this later fragmentation was more destructive. Unwittingly, the Reformation sowed the seeds of the demise of Christendom.

Not that this was obvious immediately. Europe remained officially Christian. The story and symbols of Christianity continued to permeate European culture. The partnership between church and state persisted, albeit increasingly at the level of principalities and emerging nation-states rather than empire. And challenges to the Christendom system by Anabaptists and others, though worrying, were not yet powerful enough to threaten the status quo.

But a century of religious warfare between the mini-Christendoms, with the aims and arms of all sides blessed by church leaders, and the rise of further dissident movements that rejected state control of the churches, severely weakened Christendom. In time, as the impact of the eighteenth-century movement known as the Enlightenment swept away former loyalties and certainties, many Europeans would turn away from Christianity in favor of a secular society. But before that option was popular, many would abandon the state-church synthesis and pursue the "free church" course that Anabaptists had pioneered.

By the middle of the twentieth century, it was becoming clear in Europe that Christendom was in terminal decline. The term *post-Christendom* began to appear as observers wondered what might succeed 1,500 years of European history. Some state churches still persist in Europe, but these now seem anachronistic, and from time to time proposals are made to sever the links.[2] Active participation in churches of almost all traditions has dropped significantly, with some major denominations facing extinction during the first half of the present century. The Christian story is becoming unfamiliar; Christian symbols are no longer recognized; and churches no longer occupy the cultural center in most western societies.

I collect post-Christendom anecdotes—stories that illustrate the demise of Christendom and the increasing unfamiliarity of (especially younger) people in western societies with the Christian story and its symbols. Here are three recent examples:

- *From Denmark.* In a church service, bread for communion had been broken into small pieces and put on a plate. A visitor asked whether this was meant for the birds and would be put outside after the service.

- *From the Czech Republic.* A girl looked at a picture of the crucifixion in an art gallery and asked, "Who did that to him?" Her friend responded, "It was the Communists."[3]

- *From England.* Walking past a church building on the way to school, a young boy asked his mother who the figure was on a crucifix. She didn't know and asked later at the school's coffee time if anyone else did. Only one of the twenty-five parents knew the answer.

Anomalies, vestiges of former glory, the persistence of civil religion, rearguard actions, predictions of imminent revival, and efforts to persuade people to come "back to church" cannot disguise the reality that Christendom is disappearing and a new landscape is becoming visible. It is this landscape, with so few familiar features, that many western Christians find threatening, bleak, and disorientating. What does it mean to be a follower of Jesus today? How can the churches sustain themselves and engage with a society that has marginalized their influence? What does mission mean in a context where there are many religious options competing with secularism for the hearts and minds of our contemporaries?

These questions concern all western Christians today.[4] And quick and easy answers cannot be trusted. We will not find a new program or strategy that will solve all our problems. Nor will doggedly doing what we have always done, or perhaps trying even harder, bring back what we feel we have lost. We are in the throes of a major culture shift the like of which we have not experienced for many generations.

So why are Anabaptists inclined to celebrate the end of Christendom?

- Because we are not convinced that Christendom was authentically Christian; there were wonderful Christian people and institutions in Christendom, but the Christendom shift, we believe, was a tragic mistake, and the system it produced was fundamentally flawed and deeply unchristian.

- Because we believe authentic faith and discipleship flourish in contexts where choosing not to believe carries no social sanctions. Once inducements, coercion, and cultural pressure have disappeared, what remains is more likely to be true Christian faith.

- Because we believe that Christendom marginalized Jesus and distorted the gospel. Its demise is an opportunity to restore Jesus to the center of the Christian faith and to rediscover the transformative potential of the gospel in all aspects of life.

This does not mean that grieving the end of Christendom is inappropriate. There are real losses as well as gains. We can look back with gratitude and appreciation, as well as with horror and dismay, at the Christendom era. But once we have paid our respects, it is surely time for some "post-Christendom parties"! Imperial Christianity is finished; may God lead us on into the new adventure that post-Christendom represents.[5]

WHAT IS POST-CHRISTENDOM?

In the first volume of the After Christendom series, I proposed a definition of post-Christendom that seems to have met with widespread acceptance: "the culture that emerges as the Christian faith loses coherence within a society that has been definitively shaped by the Christian story and as the institutions that have been developed to express Christian convictions decline in influence."[6] The same book suggested that the shift from Christendom to post-Christendom can be interpreted by reference to seven transitions:

- *From the center to the margins*: in Christendom the Christian story and the churches were central, but in post-Christendom these are marginal.

- *From majority to minority*: in Christendom Christians comprised the (often overwhelming) majority, but in post-Christendom we are a minority.

- *From settlers to sojourners*: in Christendom Christians felt at home in a culture shaped by their story, but in post-Christendom we are aliens, exiles, and pilgrims in a culture where we no longer feel at home.

- *From privilege to plurality*: in Christendom Christians enjoyed many privileges, but in post-Christendom we are one community among many in a plural society.

- *From control to witness*: in Christendom the churches could exert control over society, but in post-Christendom we exercise influence only through witnessing to our story and its implications.

- *From maintenance to mission*: in Christendom the emphasis was on maintaining a supposedly Christian status quo, but in post-Christendom it is on mission within a contested environment.

- *From institution to movement*: in Christendom the churches operated mainly in institutional mode, but in post-Christendom we must become again a Christian movement.[7]

I have presented these transitions in hundreds of places, suggesting that the first five are happening whether we like them or not and that the last two represent challenges we face if we are to respond effectively. Reactions to these transitions have been varied, but nowhere have they been dismissed as inaccurate or inconsequential. Post-Christendom is a reality that western Christians recognize, even if this term is new to some.

What reactions have I encountered? Here are three popular responses:

- "We recognize the reality you are describing, but we don't want to embrace it. Can we not find a way to restore Christendom?"

- "Our church has never been part of the Christendom system. Might God be raising us and others like us up to replace Christendom?"

- "We do not believe the future will look like this. God will not allow it. There will be a revival that will turn our society back to God."

I have not been persuaded that any of these reactions is helpful. I do not believe there is any way back to Christendom, nor do I want to see this flawed system restored. I accept that some newer churches feel unconnected to the Christendom era, but most are infected with the Christendom virus and, given the chance, would simply reinvent Christendom. And I suspect that much talk of revival is shot through with Christendom assumptions and expectations—not least that western Christians are God's favorites and so Christian faith in the West cannot possibly become marginal.

Anabaptists, in common with some Christians in other traditions, are drawn to a different response to these transitions. What if the western churches are entering a period of exile? What if God is leading us out of Christendom so that we can encounter afresh the gospel, which Christendom distorted, and Jesus, whom Christendom marginalized? What if there are resonances (if not exact parallels) between our experience today and that of the Israelite exiles in Babylon to whom Jeremiah wrote?

Rather than hankering to go back to Jerusalem, despairing of the future or becoming apathetic, Jeremiah urged them to accept their new situation as the will of God, to seek God's blessing on those they perceived as their enemies, and to act creatively in ways that would sustain their own community (Jeremiah 29:1-9).

With hindsight we recognize that exile was profoundly significant for the Israelites. Their vision of God expanded hugely: God was God in Babylon as well as in Israel, the God of all the earth. The perennial issue of idolatry was finally dealt with. The emergence of the synagogue in a context where there was no longer access to the temple transformed their religious life—and would influence the shape and practices of the early churches. Prophetic insights into God's intentions for humanity, culminating in new heavens and a new earth, were woven into their Scriptures, which were collected, edited, and reapplied in this new situation. Might a period of "exile" for western Christians today be equally transformative, liberating, and envisioning? Can we not discern the hand of God in this?

This does not mean that post-Christendom will be an easy environment for Christian faith and discipleship. The very mixed legacy of the Christendom era, Anabaptists suggest, has left us ill equipped for the challenges ahead. But there are also wonderful opportunities if we have the eyes to see them and the courage to grasp them.

Maybe it is easier for Christians in the Anabaptist tradition to adopt this perspective. The seven transitions summarized above require a very significant paradigm shift for churches that have a history of centrality and majority status, Christians who have felt settled and secure, and denominations used to exercising influence if not control, unaccustomed to engaging with others on a level playing field. Transitioning from an institutional ethos to a movement mentality and setting maintenance in the context of mission (rather than vice versa) will require determination, patience, and constant monitoring if the default position is not to reassert itself.

But Anabaptists have almost always been in the minority, on the margins, operating in a contested environment, unable to exercise control even if they had wished to, and perceiving themselves as resident aliens. At times they have settled for maintenance rather than mission and have become enmeshed in institutionalism, but "movement" and "mission" have been at the heart of the Anabaptist movement.

So the Anabaptist heritage of operating on the margins of Christendom means that this tradition has distinctive contributions to make as western Christians from all traditions move from grieving the end of Christendom to celebrating at post-Christendom parties. What can the Anabaptist tradition bring to these parties?

- *A call to repentance.* It is not enough simply to acknowledge that Christendom is fading and to make the necessary adjustments. If we are to seize the opportunities of post-Christendom, we need to disavow those aspects of Christendom that have distorted the gospel, alienated our society, and continue to disable us.

- *A warning about ideology.* Christendom was more than a geographical region, a historical era, or a political arrangement. Christendom was a mindset, an ideology. And this way of construing how God acts in the world, this constellation of values and expectations, will persist long after other aspects of Christendom have gone. It may also reappear in new forms in other parts of the world.[8]

- *A challenge to detox.* The Christendom era has left the body of Christ with toxins in its bloodstream—practices, instincts, commitments, structures, attitudes, biases, compromises, and reactions that damage our health and disfigure our witness. We need to purge these toxins from our system.

- *A plea to divest.* Scattered across church and society are vestiges of Christendom—numerous practices, institutions, privileges, reflexes, attitudes, ways of speaking and thinking—that are not only outdated and inappropriate in a plural society but are often unjust and a hindrance to mission. We need to divest ourselves of these and learn different ways of thinking and acting in post-Christendom.

But these do not sound like particularly attractive party gifts. What else can Anabaptists bring?

- *Dissident practices.* For nearly five centuries, Anabaptists have been exploring ways of following Jesus and building Christian communities that are not in thrall to Christendom assumptions. As we will see in the next chapter, some of these practices predate the sixteenth century and recur in many dissident movements.

- *Unexpected insights.* Removing the Christendom blinders allows us to look at all kinds of issues—theological, ethical, ecclesial, missional—in fresh ways. One of the things that has attracted many Christians to Anabaptism has been its capacity to challenge conventional ways of thinking and stimulate imaginative thinking.

- *Marginal experience.* Traditions that have been used for political influence, social status, and cultural centrality are finding the end of Christendom uncomfortable and discouraging. Anabaptists have always been on the margins, so the demise of Christendom is much less disorientating. Rather than bemoaning loss of influence, Anabaptists revel in opportunities to reconnect with the biblical story in which the kingdom of God seems normally to advance in unexpected and marginal places.

- *Peaceful witness.* Post-Christendom is a contested environment. Our calling is to bear witness to Jesus Christ in a plural society with competing interest groups and a persistent risk of social fragmentation. Some are tempted to withdraw and keep silent (historically some Anabaptists have succumbed to this temptation). Others are tempted to act belligerently, defend any remaining privileges, and impose their views on others. Anabaptism, at its best, offers a model of peaceful witness that integrates words and deeds, personal and communal testimony, listening and speaking.

- *The centrality of Jesus.* We have already explored this Anabaptist emphasis in the previous chapter. It is the insistence on the centrality of Jesus that may well be the Anabaptists' greatest gift to post-Christendom Christians.

As representatives of a broader and older dissenting tradition, Anabaptists bring to these parties not only a trenchant critique of Christendom but an alternative interpretation and embodiment of Christian discipleship. There are other ways of being Christian, building Christian communities, and sharing Christian faith than those with which the mainstream traditions have been familiar. Other traditions will bring their own gifts, some rescued from the dying embers of Christendom, others imported from regions of the world that Christendom did not reach. Post-Christendom will require the gifts of many traditions if we are to seize the opportunities it offers.

The frequent association of the church with status, wealth, and force is inappropriate for followers of Jesus and damages our witness. We are committed to exploring ways of being good news to the poor, power-less, and persecuted, aware that such discipleship may attract opposi-tion, resulting in suffering and sometimes ultimately martyrdom.

CHRISTENDOM MEANT COLLUSION

The most visible legacies of the Christendom era in Europe are the cathedrals, basilicas, and parish churches in which worshippers have gathered Sunday after Sunday over many centuries. These build-ings bear the imprint of the generations that have worshipped in them. They are places where people have prayed and sung, grieved and celebrated, sat quietly and stood reverently. For many visitors they are sacred spaces where God seems closer than usual and prayer comes more naturally. They also teach theology and retell the Chris-tian story through architecture, stained glass, tapestries, paintings, sculptures, icons, and mosaics.

In many rural areas, these buildings are in the center of the community and still dominate the skyline; in most cities, they are now dwarfed and overshadowed by office buildings and high-rise apartments. As Christendom fades, some continue to be centers of spiritual life and precious community spaces, but others are visited mainly by tourists now, and many parish churches have been con-verted into warehouses, apartments, museums, or meeting places for other faith communities.

Many of these buildings also reflect the values and assumptions of the Christendom era. They are designed for audiences to watch and listen to the clergy performing, rather than for community participation. Their size and grandeur may be intended to convey a sense of the awesomeness of God, but they also underline the social status of the church. Their adornment with costly materials and the sheer expense of building and maintaining them may be intended to glorify God, but this also reflects the wealth of the church and the choices its leaders have made about how to use their resources. And in many church buildings are regimental flags and memorials to those who have died in wars, reminding us how deeply implicated the church has been in sanctifying lethal violence.

Historic church buildings make visible the glories and compromises of Christendom. The conversion of Constantine prompted a massive construction program as imperial funds were made available to create places of worship fit for an imperial religion. Patterned on the most impressive civic buildings of the day, the new basilicas and cathedrals provided spaces for huge congregations. No longer would small churches meet in tenement blocks, adapted private homes, or wherever they could gather without fear of discovery. Splendid church buildings soon outshone all other architectural achievements. Positioned centrally and proliferating across Europe, they demonstrated unmistakably the final triumph of the gospel over paganism. But they also embodied the church's collusion with status, wealth, and force that many today find so unpalatable.

The early Anabaptists were deeply troubled by this collusion. As a movement of mainly poor, powerless, and persecuted followers of Jesus, they were no doubt unusually sensitive to this issue. The exorbitant wealth of the church and its exaction of tithes from those who could ill afford such payments seemed utterly inconsistent with the example and teaching of Jesus, whose mandate was to bring good news to the poor (Luke 4:18-20). The lordly status of bishops, the identification of the church with the interests of the powerful, and its reluctance to challenge or change an unjust and oppressive social system were difficult to square with the subversive message of the gospel, in which the lowly would be exalted and the powerful brought low (1:52). And the complicity of the church in the use of violence and force by the state—whether in warfare, crusades, executions, torture, inquisition, or persecution—deeply distressed those who heard Jesus urging the love of enemies and the renunciation of violence and coercion.

Anabaptists today share these concerns. These were surely inevitable consequences of the Christendom shift. Rather than the gospel transforming the empire, imperial values and practices subverted the church. The early churches were far from perfect, as is evident in the New Testament and subsequent writings, but they did advocate and practice forms of discipleship that enabled their members to disassociate themselves from concerns about status, excessive wealth, and the use of force.

Christian communities during the first three centuries were distinctive in the ways they handled money, overturned status distinctions, and rejected the recourse to violence. Like the early Anabaptists, they were comprised in large measure of the poor, powerless, and persecuted. But the Christendom shift changed this and resulted in the collusion with status, wealth, and force that distorted the gospel the church preached and damaged its testimony to Jesus.

The association of the church with status, wealth, and force continues to alienate people from the gospel. Despite its reduced size and influence, many still perceive the church as a reactionary institution that embodies and promotes establishment values—concerned about social order rather than social justice. Many churches and denominations are still wealthy property owners and are much stronger in affluent areas than poor communities. Although the church may no longer be able to coerce those with whom it disagrees, it still often speaks and acts as if it occupies the moral high ground and can dictate to the rest of society. The strong impression is that the loss of status, wealth, and the power to exercise control is a result of historical circumstances, not renunciation or repentance.

POST-CHRISTENDOM OFFERS OPPORTUNITY

The coming of post-Christendom, however, offers the churches an opportunity to repent of these associations and to recover our calling to follow Jesus in becoming good news to the poor, powerless, and persecuted. Some of the transitions we identified earlier in this chapter can help us on this journey.

- *From the center to the margins.* A marginal church can return to its roots in the story of a God who so often works through the poor and the powerless. Rather than the top-down strategies of Christendom, Scripture reveals the bottom-up approach that characterizes God's mission. The post-Christendom church can choose to adopt such strategies and to associate with others on the margins.

- *From majority to minority.* A minority church can recover its prophetic mandate. In the Christendom era, the church had so much invested in the status quo it was hard to be prophetic or to differentiate between a supposedly Christian society and the coming kingdom of God. The post-Christendom church can rediscover hope—a vision of what society will be like when the kingdom is fully present—and advocate on behalf of those who are oppressed by the current system.

- *From settlers to sojourners.* A church in exile, a pilgrim church, can see more clearly than a church that is settled and secure. Peter addressed early Christians as *paroikoi* (resident aliens; see 1 Peter 2:11) scattered through the empire, members of various towns, cities, and provinces, but whose primary loyalty was toward the kingdom of God. In the Christendom era, the *paroikoi* became parishioners, oblivious to the persistent tension between gospel and culture. The post-Christendom church can develop counter-cultural reflexes on issues where we have compromised and colluded.

- *From privilege to plurality.* A church without privileges can better appreciate how the poor, powerless, and persecuted feel and can pursue justice for all, instead of serving its own self-interest. Rather than hankering after the lost status of Christendom or desperately trying to protect any remaining privileges that are unjust in a plural society and a hindrance to mission, the post-Christendom church can revel in its freedom from associating with status, wealth, and force and can welcome this plural environment as a much healthier context in which to share faith and work for peace and justice.

- *From control to witness.* A church that knows it can no longer control how history will turn out, what people believe, or how they behave can revert to its original calling to bear witness to the gospel. In the Christendom era, the church invested enormous energy in exercising social and religious control, persecuting dissidents, and imposing its will on the poor and the powerless. Recognizing that these days are gone and renouncing such oppressive policies, the post-Christendom church can instead invest all its energies in living out the gospel in ways

that really are good news to the poor and inviting others to follow the One who inspires such ways of living.

LEARNING AND EXPLORING

The two core convictions we have unpacked in this chapter commit us to learning and exploring. Anabaptists today are certainly
not claiming to know in advance what post-Christendom will look
like or how to respond to the challenges it will present. We want
to learn from the Anabaptist tradition (and the broader dissenting
tradition that includes Waldensians, Lollards, the Czech Brethren,
Moravians, early Baptists, and others). We hope and expect that
the experience of those who rejected the Christendom system long
before it disintegrated might inspire and guide us as we live among
its ruins and move out into post-Christendom. And we want to
explore ways of disavowing the associations of the past that have
compromised our witness and discover what it means to be good
news to and among those on the margins of our society.

Urban Expression, mentioned in chapter 1, is a mission agency
with Anabaptist values. Its mandate is to plant new churches in poor,
urban communities, not by imposing forms of church from elsewhere
but by discovering authentic ways of incarnating the gospel in these
diverse communities. Why prioritize poor, inner-city communities?
Because it is in these communities that the reality of post-Christendom is most apparent, so exploring what the good news means here
and learning what church looks like here is strategic. If we do not
explore and learn in these communities, we will struggle elsewhere as
post-Christendom advances across our culture. But a more fundamental reason is simply the commitment spelled out in this fourth core
conviction: "exploring ways of being good news to the poor."

Urban Expression also has its own core commitments, which
are rooted in the Anabaptist tradition. Here are two of them:

• We are committed to following God on the margins and in
the gaps, expecting to discover God at work among powerless
people and in places of weakness.

• We are committed to unconditional service, holistic ministry, bold proclamation, prioritizing the poor, and being a voice for the voiceless.[9]

Being a "voice for the voiceless" is also at the heart of Speak, another Anabaptist-oriented agency mentioned in chapter 1. The founding vision of this community, which campaigns and prays for social justice, is to "speak out for those who cannot speak, for the rights of all the destitute" (Proverbs 31:8).[10]

Many other agencies and congregations are involved in similar and far more impressive initiatives, drawing on many different theological and spiritual resources. The Anabaptist tradition is only one of these resources, and we are certainly not claiming that it is the most influential, although its impact is growing and we believe that it has a distinctive contribution to make. But this fourth core conviction commits us to joining a growing movement of Christians who are exploring ways of being good news to the poor as Christendom fades.

The transition from Christendom to post-Christendom is ongoing. We believe learning and exploring are appropriate responses and commitments for Anabaptists and other Christians today as we journey into an emerging culture that is still taking shape. This commitment to the poor and powerless—and the open-endedness involved in learning and exploring rather than having all the answers—recall us again to the vulnerability implied by the phrase "the naked Anabaptist."

That vulnerability is expressed even more starkly in the final sentence of the fourth core conviction: "We are committed to exploring ways of being good news to the poor, powerless, and persecuted, aware that such discipleship may attract opposition, resulting in suffering and sometimes ultimately martyrdom." For early Anabaptists, discipleship always meant costly action and the threat of opposition and suffering. In the sixteenth century, thousands were executed, often after terrible tortures, and many more were imprisoned, exiled, flogged, separated from their families, and deprived of their homes and meager possessions. Suffering and persecution was no surprise to them. They had read in 2 Timothy 3:12 that "all who want to live a godly life in Christ Jesus will be persecuted," and in many other texts that suffering was likely for true followers of Jesus, so they accepted this as normal. This treatment also convinced them that the Christendom system was anti-Christian and that the persecuting state churches could not be truly Christian.

Including a reference to opposition, suffering, and even martyrdom in this core conviction may seem strange, even ludicrous, in a statement intended for western Christians. There is no apparent prospect of such treatment in liberal, secular societies that pride themselves on tolerance. What would one have to do to be persecuted, let alone martyred, in Britain today? From time to time Christians complain about restrictions placed on them at work or object to being required to collude in activities that go against their convictions, but the opposition and suffering in such incidents is so minor that it should not be described as persecution. And quite often Christians unnecessarily attract opposition by trying to cling to Christendom privileges, promoting our own interests rather than pursuing justice for all, or failing to display a sense of humor and proportion. This is not persecution.

But western Christians are members of a global church. Many members of this church in other parts of the world are suffering persecution because of their faithful discipleship and witness to Jesus Christ. Significant numbers have been martyred in recent years. If nothing else, including this sentence in our core convictions reminds Anabaptists today of our heritage and of our solidarity with the suffering church throughout the world.

Might post-Christendom eventually result in opposition, suffering, and even martyrdom for western Christians? This is not implausible. Already, tensions between different faith communities in Britain have resulted in the serious persecution of those who convert and those who are regarded as responsible for this. Secularists, frustrated by the persistence of religion and the resurgence of spirituality in societies that were supposed to be growing out of such immaturity, are becoming increasingly belligerent. If any of the threats to our affluent western way of life that are already on the horizon become acute, measures taken in the name of security might indeed threaten the civil liberties of any who challenge or oppose the status quo. If the post-

Christendom church identifies with the poor, powerless, and perse-cuted—often the scapegoats in times of crisis—followers of Jesus might find themselves suffering with them.

In any case, how do we interpret that troubling verse in 2 Timothy: "Everyone who wants to live a godly life in Christ Jesus will be perse-cuted"? Rather than asking whether or not persecution is feasible in western societies today, maybe we should be asking why we are not being persecuted. Are we still under the sheltering wing of a fading Christendom? Or are we simply not living as faithful disciples and so not worth persecuting? That might be the question early Anabaptists would ask us to ponder.

5

Community and Discipleship

THE DEMISE of Christendom and the gradual emergence of a culture we can only name at this point as "post-Christendom" pose many questions for the church in western societies. We have already reflected on some of these. With whom do churches primarily identify and express solidarity? How do we disavow our long association with status, wealth, and power? What new opportunities does post-Christendom offer? How do we respond to the challenge of becoming missional communities with the capacity to thrive in an emerging culture?

The fifth core conviction invites us to probe more deeply into the nature and dynamics of Christian community. What kinds of churches can respond creatively and courageously to this changing environment? If the legacy of the Christendom era is ambivalent at best and deeply problematic in many areas, can the Anabaptist tradition offer fresh perspectives?

Churches are called to be committed communities of discipleship and mission, places of friendship, mutual accountability, and multivoiced worship. As we eat together, sharing bread and wine, we sustain hope as we seek God's kingdom together. We are committed to nurturing and developing such churches, in which young and old are valued, leadership is consultative, roles are related to gifts rather than gender, and baptism is for believers.

It is not surprising at a time of cultural upheaval and uncertainty (of which the transition from Christendom to post-Christendom is only one aspect) that Christians across western societies are wrestling with what it means to be church today. Many readers will be very familiar with phrases such as "new ways of being church," "emerging church," and "fresh expressions of church." Some may be involved in these ecclesial experiments; others may be watching with interest, hope, or concern. Some of these emerging churches are clear about what they believe church should be; others are on journeys of discovery, unsure as yet what they will become. Some are motivated by mission, especially within neglected networks and neighborhoods; others are yearning for authentic expressions of worship and community, and are serving Christians who are struggling with inherited forms of church.[1]

Still others respond to the question "What does it mean to be church?" by questioning the central role of congregational meetings characteristic of the Christendom churches. For some, this means paring back the complexities of church life in order to discover "simple church"—developing sustainable and reproducible expressions of Christian community in an era with fewer resources to maintain cumbersome institutions. Others argue that even simple churches are still wedded to meetings and advocate liquid forms of community or "church beyond the congregation." Others suggest that more—rather than less—committed forms of community will be essential in a culture that offers less support for discipleship. They propose new expressions of monasticism.[2]

But most Christians continue to participate, enthusiastically or reluctantly, in expressions of church that have been inherited from the Christendom era. Indeed, the largest and most vibrant churches are traditional in style, conservative in doctrine, autocratic or managerial in leadership style, patriarchal, and institutional. Many of these churches look with disdain at the fragile communities emerging alongside them, seeing no need to take cognizance of the end of Christendom or to adapt more than pragmatically for a changing culture. And cathedrals all over England (the most impressive vestiges of former Christendom glories) are reporting increased attendances.

It will be some time before we can judge whether the current wave of emerging churches and fresh expressions of church will result in sustainable and missionally potent forms of community. It will be some time, too, before we know whether the apparently successful inherited churches are serving the last generation for whom Christendom is their natural habitat and providing refuge for those who yearn for certainty and stability in a period of flux, or whether these communities can evolve in ways that will enable them to engage with a wider range of people in a post-Christendom society. A time of transition calls for provisionality and generosity, rather than dogmatism and competition. Furthermore, post-Christendom is likely to be too diverse for any one expression of church to be adequate. Inherited and emerging churches may need to embrace each other in a new missionary ecumenism if we are to discover what it means to be "church after Christendom."

ANABAPTISM: AN EMERGING CHURCH MOVEMENT

What contribution might the Anabaptist tradition make to this missionary ecumenism and to the search for ways of being "church after Christendom" that are contextually sensitive and consistent with biblical values and practices?

Early Anabaptism was an emerging church movement. Despite its very different cultural context, it has significant resonances with the contemporary scene. If you are familiar with emerging churches today, compare them with these characteristics:

- Anabaptist churches emerged at a time of social, political, economic, cultural, and religious turmoil when questions of authority and authenticity were on the agenda.

- Anabaptism was not a single movement but emerged from numerous experiments in various places as pioneers gradually discovered others with similar passions.

- Anabaptist communities developed in divergent ways and sometimes disagreed strongly with the decisions and practices of other communities.

- Anabaptists made use of emerging technology (printing rather than the internet) to disseminate their ideas and connect with each other.

- Many members of Anabaptist churches had been disillusioned by their experience in inherited churches and by the failure of these churches to transform society.

- Anabaptist communities welcomed the opportunity to explore alternative models and patterns of church life, free from ecclesial restrictions.

- Many Anabaptist churches rejected the "performance mentality" of other churches and encouraged multivoiced church life.

- Some contemporaries called the Anabaptists "the new monastics"[3] because of their emphasis on discipleship and accountable community.

- Anabaptism was at heart a missionary movement, concerned not only about new ways of being church but also about personal and social transformation.

- Anabaptist churches offered alternatives to the dominant Christendom expression of church.

Some emerging churches today, recognizing points of contact, are already drawing on the Anabaptist tradition for inspiration and guidance. Several commentators on the emerging church scene have noted similarities, which may encourage more pioneers to investigate this tradition. Anabaptism is a natural and stimulating conversation partner for emerging churches. This may become even more apparent when emerging churches understand and interpret their context as post-Christendom as well as postmodern.

An emerging church with explicit Anabaptist values is Peacechurch in Birmingham, England.[4] Joe and Sarah Baker, who host this community, are connected with the Workshop course and with Urban Expression, as well as the Anabaptist Network. The church website explains how Anabaptist perspectives have shaped the community. Other Peacechurch groups are emerging in Bristol, Coventry, and elsewhere. What kind of church emerges if peace (or shalom) is the core value?

Other emerging churches were represented at a conference the Anabaptist Network ran (in partnership with the Northumbria Community) in May 2008, entitled "New Habits for a New Era," exploring ways of learning from the monastic tradition and reappropriating its resources in a new cultural context. With input from a Franciscan monk, Anabaptists, and members of the Northumbria Community, who draw on Celtic and other expressions of monasticism, this was a stimulating day of cross-fertilizing and learning together.

If nothing else, then, Anabaptism may encourage emerging churches that they are not the first to ask the kinds of questions they are asking or to need space to explore fresh ways of being church. But the Anabaptist tradition offers two additional perspectives.

First, as a tradition that developed on the fringes of Christendom, in conscious opposition to some of the beliefs, structures, priorities, and practices of the Christendom churches, Anabaptism offers an unusual historical reference point for those who are searching for ways of being church after Christendom. Just because emerging churches espouse values or develop practices that sixteenth-century Anabaptists pioneered does not validate them, but this might reassure those who suspect emerging churches of being unduly influenced by postmodern culture.

Second, early Anabaptists were actually less concerned about fitting in with their culture than about recovering neglected biblical practices, regardless of the social consequences. Some emerging churches may find this salutary, challenging their tendency to prioritize cultural attunement over counter-cultural faithfulness.

But, as we investigate the fifth core conviction, it is worth noting that inherited churches from many traditions are also learning from Anabaptism. As Christendom disintegrates, many of these churches recognize that they need to reimagine what it is to be church. As they respond to this challenge, their journeys might be described as "evolving" rather than "emerging." There are different dynamics involved. But they are encountering many of the same issues and often exploring similar possibilities. It is essential that inherited and emerging churches learn from one another as post-Christendom advances. Perhaps shared interest in the Anabaptist tradition can help us all communicate.

COMMUNITIES OF DISCIPLESHIP AND MISSION

Anabaptists are not unique in understanding of churches as a "committed communities of discipleship and mission," or at least in aspiring to this. As with many aspects of this core conviction and of others, the Anabaptist tradition articulates what numerous Christians throughout the centuries and from many traditions have believed and longed for. But the contribution of Anabaptism to this now widespread conviction is often underestimated. It may be unremarkable today to suggest that discipleship and mission are key components in church life, but Anabaptists were mocked and persecuted for daring to suggest this.

Throughout the Christendom era, "churchgoing" was an accurate description of how most people participated. Church was a sacred building they visited regularly or periodically, an event organized by professionals at which they were mainly passive spectators, or an institution to which they had belonged since infancy and to which they could look when necessary for certain services. Church membership and civic membership were closely interrelated. "Going to church" was one of many activities shared with one's neighbors.

Few churchgoers during this era understood themselves to be participants in the mission of God or thought of the church as a missional community. The language of mission was not familiar (indeed *mission* was primarily a theological term describing the sending of the Son by the Father, rather than a task in which churchgoers might share). There was no apparent need for mission within Christendom, for almost all were already Christian, and society, while far from perfect, was under the rule of Christ as mediated by the leaders of church and state. Mission was, of course, necessary beyond the borders of Christendom, but that was the responsibility of the state and of specialist agencies.

A problematic legacy of Christendom is separation between "mission" and "community." Sustained efforts by many denominations and local churches to reunite these estranged partners, using the language of "missionary congregations," "mission-shaped church," "missional church," or several other such phrases, have been only partially effective. The division between mission and community is deep-rooted, institutionally entrenched, and resilient to change. For many church members, mission is an activity of specialists and is mainly necessary in other places.

Some advocates of churches as "missionary communities" point to the early Anabaptists as an example of what they mean. Like most of their contemporaries, Anabaptists had little knowledge of, or interest in, the world beyond Christendom; but, unlike most of their contemporaries, they regarded Europe as a mission field. Christendom, they said, was not genuinely Christian. Their friends and neighbors needed to be converted. Their society needed to be transformed by the gospel. Stories abound of uneducated but passionate evangelists sharing their faith with family, friends, and neighbors; community members sent out two by two to plant new churches; and traveling salesmen preaching the gospel as they hawked their wares from town to town.

Hans Nadler was a needle seller. As he traveled around Europe, Nadler would strike up conversations with people. According to court testimony, "whenever he met goodhearted persons in inns or on the street . . . he would give instruction from the Word of God" and would outline how his hearers could "be born anew." Nadler was illiterate but developed an approach based on line-by-line expositions of the Lord's Prayer and the Apostles' Creed, which could be understood by virtually everyone, educated and uneducated alike.[5]

The Great Commission (Matthew 28:18-20), which would inspire global mission in the following centuries, was embraced by Anabaptists in the sixteenth century as a biblical mandate, not only for baptizing believers rather than infants, but also for their missionary endeavors.

Not all Anabaptists have been as enthusiastic about mission as the first generation. The impact of sustained persecution, among other factors, resulted in many communities in the latter part of the sixteenth century agreeing to keep quiet about their faith and to focus on faithful living rather than bold witness. This legacy continues to discourage many of their direct descendants from overt evangelism, although other aspects of mission—not least relief work and many forms of social action—have flourished. But the struggle to reestablish a "missional church" identity among contemporary Anabaptists continues.

If the self-designation *missionary* would not have come naturally to most churchgoers in the Christendom era, nor would *disciple*—especially if this term implied more than attending church and conforming to social and cultural norms. Higher standards of ethical behavior and greater spiritual achievements were expected from the clergy and monastic communities (although sadly these were not always evident), but discipleship was not for "ordinary" Christians.

Anabaptists, like earlier dissident and renewal movements, protested about this state of affairs. Disappointed by the failure of the Reformation to inspire significant behavioral change in church or society, they opted to plant new churches in which commitment and discipleship were expected. The reformers abolished the two-tier Christendom system by dismantling the monastic communities but, according to the Anabaptists, failed to teach and practice Christian discipleship. The Anabaptist approach was to abolish the two-tier system by calling all followers of Jesus to be disciples (one of the reasons Anabaptists were dubbed "new monastics").

Significant theological differences were at the root of disagreements between Anabaptists and the reformers on the nature of the church and expectations of discipleship:

- The reformers understood *grace* to mean the justification of sinners through the work of Christ; Anabaptists interpreted *grace* as the transforming power of God at work in those who have been justified.

- The reformers were concerned to avoid any suspicion of "salvation by works" and to emphasize God's sovereign initiative in salvation; Anabaptists rejected the doctrine of predestination and what they perceived as "faith without works" in the reformers' churches.

- The reformers retained the territorial understanding of church inherited from Christendom and the expectation of a "mixed" community; Anabaptists planted churches comprised of those who committed themselves to be disciples.

What Anabaptists were pioneering in the sixteenth century were fresh expressions of church. This was the beginning of the "free church" movement that has proliferated into multiple networks and denominations, united by their conviction that membership is by choice, not birth, and that *all* church members are called to be disciples. This model of church is now taken for granted in many traditions, but it emerged out of great suffering and courageous resistance.

Anabaptists today are committed to nurturing and developing such churches; churches in which *both* discipleship *and* mission are understood as core commitments. Emerging and inherited churches, as chapter 3 indicated, are wrestling with the relationship between "belonging," "believing," and "behaving." In a postmodern culture of suspicion and a post-Christendom context where the Christian story is unfamiliar, many people need longer to decide if they want to become followers of Jesus. Journeying with communities that are open-edged and welcoming, that do not pressurize them to believe or behave in certain ways, has been essential for many who are exploring the Christian faith.

This was true for Bernard. His wife belonged to the Wood Green Mennonite Church, but Bernard was not a believer. He was a Jew and an agnostic. But over the years he watched and listened, developed friendships in the church, participated in various church activities, and attended more regularly than many members. The church welcomed him and waited patiently. He imbibed their values and shared his concerns, prayer requests, and, finally, prayers. One day he called God "Father." Shortly before he died, eighteen years after first attending the church, he was baptized as a believer.[6]

An Anabaptist understanding of discipleship as "following" endorses this gradual and gracious approach. But Anabaptists are wary of allowing "belonging," "believing," and "behaving" to become disconnected, fearing that such an approach would result in churches where discipleship is optional.

Anabaptist anthropologist Paul Hiebert's identification of

"bounded," "fuzzy," "open," and "centered" sets to describe different kinds of community has been enlightening to many church leaders.[7] Historically, Anabaptists and most dissident traditions have espoused the "bounded set" approach, maintaining firm boundaries and distinguishing between insiders and outsiders on the basis of belief and behavior. Today, many Anabaptists regard the "centered set" approach as more congruent with their convictions. This approach is less concerned about insiders and outsiders than the direction in which people are traveling. There is a definite center and strong core convictions that define the community, but this allows for open edges. Communities committed to both mission and discipleship find a centered set understanding helpful.

FRIENDSHIP AND MUTUAL ACCOUNTABILITY
Their contemporaries accused early Anabaptists of confusing discipleship with legalism and perfectionism. Like other discipleship-oriented movements before and since, their search for a "pure church" was dismissed as unrealistic and arrogant. Undoubtedly, at times, Anabaptists were guilty of all these charges: arrogance, perfectionism, legalism, and unrealistic expectations. But the frequent use of the term "pure church" to denigrate their aspirations surely reveals as much about the low expectations of their critics. There is a firm biblical basis for seeking a pure church and forming communities of disciples who live distinctive and attractive lives (see 2 Corinthians 11:2-3; Philippians 2:15; Revelation 19:7-8).

The early Christians frequently invited enquirers and adversaries to examine the way they lived, as individuals and communities, as evidence of the truth of their convictions and the presence of God among them. There are many reluctant testimonies from outsiders to the quality of life of the Christian communities in the first three centuries. This changed in the Christendom era. Church members became less and less distinctive, and their lives no longer attracted others to become followers of Jesus.

Theological justifications were found for a lower level of discipleship and "mixed" churches—not least an interpretation of the parable of the weeds (Matthew 13:23-30, 36-43), which was understood to mean that weeds should not be pulled up but should be allowed to grow unhindered in the church until the end of the age. Constant repetition of this interpretation means that many are surprised to discover that this parable (one of few Jesus actually interprets) specifically identifies the field in which the weeds are growing as the world, *not* the church. This distinction may have been redundant in a Christendom society where there was little real difference between church and world, but successive dissident movements insisted that the parable did not legitimize a mixed church. They believed a pure church (if not a perfect church) was desirable and achievable.

The distinction between a pure church and a perfect church is crucial. While there have been Christians and movements that espoused perfectionism (either as achievable or as already achieved), the search for a pure church does not imply this. Many critics seem unwilling or unable to appreciate this distinction. In fact, critics frequently interpret as evidence of perfectionism an Anabaptist practice—mutual accountability—that points in the opposite direction.

Various words or phrases are used to describe the practice of mutual accountability, some more winsome than others, including admonition, church discipline, the ban, the rule of Christ, and interactive pastoral care. Basing their commitment to this practice especially on the instructions of Jesus (in Matthew 18:15-17), Anabaptists insisted that mutual accountability was a third mark of the true church alongside the two recognized by the reformers (faithful preaching of the gospel and proper administration of the sacraments). It was the absence of mutual accountability, they argued, that prevented the reformers' churches from being communities of disciples; sound doctrine was not enough on its own.

In the Anabaptist tradition, mutual accountability is a resource for would-be disciples, recognizing human weakness and our need for support and correction. Early Anabaptists committed themselves to this process when they were baptized, welcoming the help of brothers and sisters as they attempted to follow Jesus. Far from endorsing perfectionist tendencies, this practice belongs in a community that yearns for purity but is all too well aware of imperfection, compromise, and unfaithfulness.

There are many reasons not to practice mutual accountability today. Individualism and a privatized approach to ethics, coupled with a woolly and uncritical notion of tolerance, make this uncongenial. Churches are rarely trained to apply the biblical teaching well and graciously, so, when occasionally pushed into action in emergency circumstances, many apply it poorly and cause further damage. This in turn discredits the practice and causes others to shy away from it. And the legacy of Christendom in this area is troubling. When church discipline was exercised, it was frequently punitive and sometimes lethal.

But mutual accountability is not only rooted in the explicit teaching of Jesus as recorded by Matthew (indeed, in the only passage in the Gospels where the term *church* is used in association with practical instructions for community life). It is taught throughout the New Testament. And the dissident tradition once more offers an alternative approach on an issue that the Christendom system distorted. Not that Anabaptists always practiced mutual accountability graciously or wisely, but at least they did not execute those who stepped out of line.

Anabaptists today, rightly cautious because of abuses in this area, nevertheless want to nurture and develop churches where mutual accountability is understood, practiced, and valued. Mutual accountability is an antidote to gossip and backbiting, a defense against factions and divisions, and a resource for spiritual growth. We are not left on our own in our struggle against failure. When relationships break down, there is a process to bring healing and restoration. Imperfect disciples and imperfect churches need this practice.

A church in northern England, which has been deeply influenced by Anabaptist values and practices, placed on the wall of its meeting place the text of Matthew 18:15-17 with a public commitment that this was how the community would respond when relationships became strained. How is a church shaped by seeing this commitment displayed publicly whenever they meet?

Coupling mutual accountability with friendship, as this fifth core conviction does, is a reminder that honest relationships are the basis for true friendship. Mutual accountability works only in a context of trust. Speaking the truth in love (Ephesians 4:15) implies a much deeper level of engagement than many churches expect or experience.

Paradoxically, or inevitably, many people in an individualistic culture yearn for such relationships. Many leave their churches because the "fellowship" on offer is insipid or institutional and falls far short of friendship.

Some have been drawn to the Anabaptist tradition because of its emphasis on community, hospitality, and friendship. It is no coincidence that many associate Anabaptism with open homes and shared meals. This core conviction envisages a church that eats together, and many Anabaptist communities do so often and enthusiastically.

Some friends of mine have planted a church in East London with Anabaptist values and a simple motto: "No eating, no meeting!" Others have been involved in "table churches," developing "table liturgies" that integrate prayer, food, conversation, biblical reflection, sharing of bread and wine in remembrance of Jesus, and even washing up together. For many Anabaptists, the kitchen or the dining table, rather than the sanctuary, is the iconic meeting place.

Anabaptists today, as in the past, fail to live up to their own and others' expectations, so the tradition offers cautionary tales as well as inspiring examples. But the insistence of the Anabaptist tradition on the practice of mutual accountability continues to encourage us to nurture the kinds of communities where relationships are strong enough for such a practice to be life-giving and liberating.

MULTIVOICED WORSHIP AND CONSULTATIVE LEADERSHIP

One of the reasons the practice of mutual accountability is frequently referred to as "church discipline" is that church leaders have often dominated this process. This was the norm in the Christendom era, when church leadership was clerical and the clergy could count on state support to enforce any sanctions on erring church members. But there is no mention of church leaders in the foundational text. Matthew 18:15-17 encourages anyone in the community to take the initiative in resolving difficulties. Presumably, if a dispute becomes public, those with leadership responsibility in the community will oversee the continuing process, but the emphasis is on mutuality and the empowerment of the whole community.

The distortion of a process of mutual accountability into an exercise of clerical power is one of many ways in which the Christendom shift silenced the community. The church in the New Testament is presented as a multivoiced community:

- When the community gathered for worship, each member contributed his gift in order to build up the whole body (Romans 12:4-8; 1 Corinthians 14:26).

- So many people wanted to make contributions in some churches that guidelines were introduced to maintain order (1 Corinthians 14:27-28, 39-40).

- Teaching was not left to one person but involved many people reflecting together on Scripture, testing what each other said, and learning as a community (Acts 15:6-21; 1 Corinthians 14:29-31; Colossians 3:16).

- Pastoral care, as we have seen, was exercised throughout the community and not restricted to designated "pastors" (Matthew 18:15-18; Acts 4:32; Romans 12:10-13; Ephesians 4:15-16; 1 Thessalonians 5:12-15).

- There were leaders in the community, but leadership teams appear to have been the norm, comprised of people with different gifts (Acts 13:1-3; Ephesians 4:11-13).

But the church in the Christendom era was profoundly monovoiced, as chapter 3 noted. The clergy spoke and the laity listened. The reformers championed the "priesthood of all believers," but in practice some were much more priestly than others. And the legacy of Christendom remains extraordinarily influential in most traditions. Efforts to introduce multivoiced practices frequently founder because churches are ill equipped and collude in their silent passivity.

The early Anabaptists were outraged by the unhealthy dependence of churches on single voices. They declared that churches where only one person spoke and everyone else was silent were not "spiritual congregations."[8] In their own communities, it was expected that many people would participate.

Many dissident groups and emerging churches have similarly reveled in the freedom to participate in ways that were not allowed in other churches. But the Christendom legacy is strong. Most groups gradually default to the mono-voiced approach that has dominated western churches for many centuries.

Anabaptists have struggled to sustain a multivoiced ethos. Vestiges of this remain, but many contemporary Anabaptist churches have succumbed to the pressure to revert to being mono-voiced. There are many sensible reasons for this; quality control, benefiting from the expertise of those who are theologically educated, and maintaining good order are three of them. But the drawbacks may outweigh the advantages: disempowering the community, quenching the Spirit, creating dependency, silencing prophetic voices, and overburdening church leaders. And the testimony of the New Testament is that multivoiced church is normal.

The fifth core conviction commits us to resist the default position we have inherited from the Christendom era and to nurture communities where many voices are heard. This also implies models and practices of leadership that are consultative. "Multivoiced" need not mean chaotic or leaderless. Leadership is one of the gifts exercised in communities that welcome and value diverse contributions. But autocratic leadership is inappropriate for such communities and inconsistent, we believe, with the example and teaching of Jesus.

Consultative leadership can be exercised in various ways. Several Anabaptist churches have developed sophisticated processes to ensure that every voice is heard and all views taken into account. These are impressive but can also be exhausting, time consuming, and very slow. Some propose "consensus" as the ideal in decision making. Consensus does not mean that everyone necessarily agrees, but that everyone recognizes that their voice has been heard and endorses the decision of the community, even if they disagree with what has been decided. Careful listening and consultation processes could be a gift from the Anabaptist tradition to many churches that are struggling with conflict, dominated by a few powerful voices, or unfamiliar with consultative approaches.

But consultative leadership needs to emphasize "leadership" as well as "consultative." If the Anabaptist tradition has been strong on the latter, it has not always been so effective at cultivating the former. Without courageous and imaginative leadership, including the skilled management of consultation processes, communities can become risk-averse and moribund. This hardly describes the early Anabaptist communities, but it is something contemporary Anabaptist churches need to avoid.

YOUNG AND OLD, WOMEN AND MEN
Developing multivoiced churches requires us to be alert to those whose contributions are often marginalized or restricted. In some societies, respect for the wisdom of older people ensures that their voices are heard and their input sought, but this has not been customary in western societies for some time. Churches can easily conform to this cultural tendency and fail to draw on the resources and insights of older members. Whether these attitudes will persist in an aging society is unclear, but churches (whose membership is generally aging more rapidly) might explore ways of ensuring that they value older members and receive their gifts.

The status of children in contemporary western societies is somewhat ambiguous, and this is mirrored in many churches. Some may feel that children are overindulged, over-protected, and accorded undue attention. The recent trend of churches appointing staff to oversee their children's ministries can be interpreted as a desperate response to evidence that churches are losing the children of their own members, let alone other children, or as a sign that the young are being valued more than in recent generations. But many children in our society, and in our churches, are neglected, abused, stigmatized, and not enabled to reach their full potential. Churches in many traditions wrestle with questions about the status of children (present or potential members of the community?) and their participation in church life (sharing in communion? taking part vocally?). Some emerging churches, including those influenced by Anabaptism, have explored the implications of placing children at the center of the church, rather than on the fringes.

How young and old relate together, listen to each other, and receive each other's insights is a further dimension of multivoiced church life. Many emerging churches are designed to engage with a specific subculture, ethnic community, relational network, or age band. Many inherited churches are similarly restricted, by default rather than design. Questions are often raised about the legitimacy and impact of such homogenous communities. We may defend them as necessary for effective and sensitive mission in a plural culture, but can we not nurture and develop churches in which diversity enriches rather than alienates, where young and old respect and serve each other?

Can the Anabaptist tradition offer any resources to help us grapple with these issues? The most intriguing expression of intergenerational community I have encountered has been in the Hutterian Bruderhof in East Sussex, England—a three-hundred-strong, common-purse community that identifies with the communitarian strand of Anabaptism. This is a community in which older members participate actively and are valued and cared for throughout their lives, and children are nurtured by the whole community, not just within nuclear family units. In the Wood Green Mennonite Church, younger members have been paired with older members, who mentor them in the faith. Anabaptists today will join with Christians from other traditions in searching for ways to affirm and learn from young and old.

In many traditions the voices of women are still silenced or restricted to certain contexts. In some of these, theological arguments and biblical interpretations intersect with cultural and personal preferences to preclude women participating in some aspects of ministry. In others, egalitarian impulses and statements of principle are not matched by practice. This is especially true in many emerging churches. Our fifth core conviction encourages us to challenge this and to nurture churches where the voices of women and men are heard and respected equally, where roles are assigned according to gift rather than gender.

Not all Anabaptist communities, past and present, would agree with this. Some, including the Hutterian Bruderhof, have clearly defined roles assigned in relation to gender rather than gift and restrict leadership to men. But many Anabaptists today reject such policies and practices as vestiges from the patriarchal culture of Christendom. They point also to the examples of early Anabaptist churches in which the contributions of women and men were encouraged in all aspects of church life and in which women often played leading roles.[9] While cultural pressures undoubtedly restricted what Anabaptist women could do, there was much greater scope for them to exercise their God-given ministries than their Catholic or Reformed counterparts enjoyed.

As with other dimensions of this fifth core conviction, Anabaptists today are certainly not claiming to be uniquely concerned about these issues or unreservedly successful in facing the challenges they present. We acknowledge the resilience of entrenched attitudes and disempowering structures, and we celebrate the sustained efforts of Christians in various traditions to transform these. But our experience has been that Anabaptist churches and agencies have been for many women places where they can flourish and where their gifts, not their gender, have determined their roles and contributions.

BAPTISM IS FOR BELIEVERS

The final phrase of this core conviction—"and baptism is for believers"—may prove a stumbling block to some readers and a disincentive to investigating Anabaptism. Other insights on the kinds of churches that might thrive as Christendom disintegrates may be attractive and applicable within many traditions, but the insistence on a particular view of baptism is problematic for those who belong to denominations and churches that baptize infants. Do we really need to include this in our core convictions?

This is a question we have pondered. The first version of our convictions did not include this statement. It was added after considerable debate at a residential conference in which we reviewed the convictions and decided to revise them in certain ways. We recognized that this statement would alienate some and could reinforce the idea that the Anabaptist movement arose primarily because of disagreements over the meaning of baptism. Some of us wondered whether it was necessary to include in a twenty-first-century statement any reference to an issue that was highly significant in the sixteenth century but no longer had the same theological or social significance.[10]

After all, the emergence of the Anabaptist movement was provoked by other factors than disagreements over baptismal practice (even though the label "Anabaptists," or "rebaptizers," came to identify the movement). Rejection of the Christendom system, an emphasis on the centrality of Jesus, the pursuit of social justice, the separation of church and state, an emphasis on discipleship and community, advocacy of peace, and the sharing of resources—these concerns were arguably much more significant than the debate about baptism. It is to the Anabaptists perspectives on these issues that many are drawn today.

But we have inserted this statement on baptism into our core convictions. Why? Because the conviction that baptism is for believers is inextricably linked to fundamental beliefs about the nature of the church in the Anabaptist tradition. The church, Anabaptists insist, is comprised of those who believe in Jesus and want to follow him. Infants and children are embraced by the church community but are not baptized until they are ready freely to choose this as a mark of owned faith and willing discipleship. For Anabaptists, believers baptism was not the central issue, but it was *the symbol of the central issue*: what does it mean to be a follower of Jesus and what kind of community nurtures such discipleship?

Anabaptists, then and now, have principled objections to the practice of infant baptism

- Despite claims to the contrary, we are not persuaded that there is a secure New Testament basis for this practice or that an analogy with circumcision helps.

- Nor are we persuaded that various ingenious theological justifications for infant baptism are anything more than attempts to legitimize a practice that was adopted for other pastoral and political reasons.

- We are convinced that infant baptism fits snugly into the ideological framework of the sacral culture of Christendom but is inappropriate for believers churches and for a post-Christendom context.

Baptism, in the Anabaptist tradition, is not only a visible expression of personal faith but a pledge of discipleship, an invitation to mutual accountability, and commitment to active participation in the church community.

Inserting this statement in our core convictions is not intended to alienate Christians from traditions that teach a different view of baptism or to discourage them from learning from other aspects of the Anabaptist tradition. Our experience is that many pick and choose the elements they find most helpful from Anabaptism without embracing the entire tradition. But, when we discussed this at our residential conference, our conclusion was that we could not with integrity exclude from our core convictions some reference to an issue that was so important to the early Anabaptists and that continues to challenge the Christendom model of church.

SHARING BREAD AND WINE

The reformers may have been united in their opposition to the Anabaptists' understanding and practice of baptism, but they were deeply divided over the issue of communion, or the Eucharist. They all rejected the traditional Catholic understanding of the Mass, but Luther and Zwingli were at loggerheads over how to interpret the sharing of bread and wine. The Anabaptists generally followed Zwingli—sharing bread and wine was seen as a simple memorial of the death of Christ. But they had little interest in the abstruse and speculative debates that were raging in many places, including the Netherlands, where their simple approach was an attractive alternative to the complexities of the "sacramentarian controversy."

Their distinctive contribution to the practice of communion was not a further theological nuance, but an insistence that sharing bread and wine together had implications for daily discipleship and the shared life of the community.

This was summed up concisely and powerfully in the "pledge of love" introduced by Swiss Anabaptist leader Balthasar Hubmaier. Although Anabaptist worship was usually informal and spontaneous, shortly before his execution Hubmaier wrote "A Form for the Supper of Christ." This gave instructions so that members of the community would think carefully about what they were doing. Just before the bread and wine were shared, the community was invited to stand together and commit themselves afresh to God and to one another. Because so many distinctive elements of Anabaptist spirituality appear in this pledge, it is worth quoting at length:

> Brothers and sisters, if you will to love God before, in, and above all things, in the power of his holy and living Word, serve him alone, honor and adore him and henceforth sanctify his name, subject your carnal and sinful will to his divine will which he has worked in you by his living Word, in life and death, then let each say individually: "I will."
>
> If you will love your neighbor and serve him with deeds of brotherly love, lay down and shed for him your life and blood, be obedient to father, mother and all authorities according to the will of God, and this in the power of our Lord Jesus Christ, who laid down and shed his flesh and blood for us, then let each say individually: "I will."
>
> If you will practice fraternal admonition toward your brothers and sisters, make peace and unity among them, and reconcile yourselves with all those whom you have offended, abandon all envy, hate, and evil will toward everyone, willingly cease all action and behavior which causes harm, disadvantage, or offense to your neighbor; if you will also love your enemies and do good to them, and exclude according to the Rule of Christ all those who refuse to do so, then let each say individually: "I will."
>
> If you desire publicly to confirm before the church this pledge of love which you have now made, through the Lord's Supper of Christ, by eating bread and drinking wine, and to testify to it in the power of the living memorial of the suffering and death of Jesus Christ our Lord, then let each say individually: "I desire it in the power of God."
>
> So eat and drink with one another in the name of God the Father, the Son, and the Holy Spirit. May God himself accord to all of us the power and the strength that we may worthily carry it out and bring it to its saving conclusion according to his divine will. May the Lord impart his grace. Amen.[11]

Early Anabaptists generally celebrated the Lord's Supper in a domestic setting, as in the early churches, which shared bread and wine in the context of a meal. In the Christendom era, this practice was forbidden and communion became detached from the meal. In some Anabaptist-oriented churches today (and in other types of churches), bread and wine are once again being shared as the community eats together.

SUSTAINING HOPE

The borderland between a fading Christendom and an emerging post-Christendom seems an uncongenial environment for church life. Many vestiges and legacies of Christendom are cluttering up the churches, distracting Christians from the opportunities of this new context. Numbers are diminishing, social influence is declining, and the prospects seem dismal. Fresh expressions of church offer glimmers of hope, but they have yet to prove they are sustainable or able to connect with many people beyond the existing Christian constituency. Some hold on to expectations of a revival that might turn the tide; others wonder if western culture is entering a dark age when faith is all but extinguished. We know that the church is growing spectacularly in other places, but what impact will this have on us? Some suggest that post-Christendom, when this culture has finally arrived, will be as wide open to the gospel as pre-Christendom societies. But will we still be here to seize this opportunity?

The Anabaptist tradition has no easy answers to these questions, but it does encourage us to celebrate, as well as grieve, the end of Christendom and to trust God, however bleak the situation may appear. If Christendom was not the kingdom of God come on earth but an illegitimate collusion with empire, then maybe we can rejoice in its demise and fix our eyes once more on the coming kingdom of justice and peace promised by the prophets.

We are in need of a post-Christendom eschatology, a vision of the future uncontaminated by imperial ideology, a hope that will sustain us through this period of uncertainty. And we need resilient churches that can "sustain hope as we seek God's kingdom together."

Eschatology was one of the more colorful aspects of Anabaptist theology. Convinced, as were most of their contemporaries, that they were living in the final generation before the return of Christ, they anticipated joyfully the climax of history and arrival of the kingdom of God. Perhaps surprisingly for a movement generally assumed to be pacifist, some were looking forward to the wrath of God being poured out on their adversaries (and not a few hoped to be personally involved in some of the smiting). Most, however, were content to leave judgment to God and hoped merely to be welcomed into the eternal kingdom after suffering persecution for the sake of Christ.

Anabaptists today find much of the sixteenth-century language and imagery unappealing, but we may do well to reflect on the ways in which hope was kept alive in the midst of great suffering and frustrated ambitions. For the early Anabaptists, their communities were signs of hope. Whatever their undoubted weaknesses, they sustained courage and vision as they reminded one another of the story of their faith, encouraged each other to remain faithful, sang and prayed together, developed counter-cultural reflexes, and passed on their faith to the next generation.

Finally, it is worth remarking that this core conviction says nothing about the structures, forms, programs, or styles churches should adopt. Perhaps too much attention in recent years has been paid to such issues. Maybe the Christendom era overcomplicated church life. Maybe church is really quite simple. The Anabaptist tradition focuses attention on values and practices that can sustain hope in God's kingdom and build communities that embody this hope. While Anabaptist churches frequently fall short of these aspirations, Anabaptism offers a robust and attractive vision of Christian community that increasing numbers of Christians in post-Christendom are finding hopeful.

6

Justice and Peace

THE ANABAPTIST tradition is often accused of being inwardly focused, church-centered, and unconcerned with social transformation. And some Anabaptist groups have been guilty as charged. But many of the early Anabaptists had been deeply involved in campaigning for social, economic, and political justice before they joined the movement and continued to pursue these concerns as Anabaptists. The authorities were in no doubt that Anabaptists were a threat to the social order and not just members of a deviant religious community. The emergence of Anabaptism in the wake of a failed but very worrying peasants' revolt,[1] in which some Anabaptist leaders had been actively involved, meant that the movement was widely perceived as a further challenge to the status quo.

The most disturbing features of Anabaptist teaching and practice were their rejection of private property and their refusal to bear arms. The issues of "provision" and "protection" are fundamental to all human societies. Those who question the legitimacy of the means chosen to ensure that their society is defended from their enemies, or who undermine the basis on which goods are exchanged, are regarded as subversive troublemakers.

Anabaptists through the centuries have not always been as forthright on these issues as their forebears. Silenced by persecution, disrupted by migration, and more recently lured by increasing wealth into accommodation with prevailing social norms, Anabaptists have sometimes abandoned these convictions, sometimes held them quietly without advocating them to others, and sometimes concentrated on nurturing churches that embodied their convictions in conscious opposition to the surrounding culture.

Our sixth and seventh core convictions indicate ways in which many Anabaptists today are interpreting and applying historic Anabaptist perspectives on questions of justice and peace in a very different social and political context. There are opportunities to advocate and pioneer alternative approaches to provision and protection without encountering the kind of persecution the early Anabaptists experienced. And, although the sanctity of private property and reliance on weaponry to defend national interests continue to form the bedrock of most societies, many people are now convinced that alternatives must be found to conventional policies that are causing immense damage to our planet and to very large numbers of its inhabitants.

> Spirituality and economics are interconnected. In an individualist and consumerist culture and in a world where economic injustice is rife, we are committed to finding ways of living simply, sharing generously, caring for creation, and working for justice.

In both the Old and the New Testaments, spirituality and economics are interwoven. The obligations of the covenant between God and Israel, spelled out in the Law, contain many detailed economic principles and practices. The prophets constantly remind the people of Israel (and especially their political leaders) that their prayers would not be heeded if they did not pursue justice. Their worship services would be offensive to God unless they cared for the poor and needy.[2]

Jesus insists that "where your treasure is, there your heart will be also" (Matthew 6:21), and the Gospels are full of parables and instructions about wealth and poverty, the use and abuse of possessions, and the demands of community. Not only are economic issues prevalent in the rest of the New Testament, but the book of Acts introduces us to the first church in Jerusalem, in which the sharing of resources was inextricably linked with faith and discipleship.

SPIRITUALITY AND ECONOMICS

The interrelationship between spirituality and economics is evident also in the churches of the first three centuries. Economic issues featured strongly in the sermons, letters, and treatises of church leaders, and in the teaching of those who were entering the churches. Entrenched social inequality was not immediately overturned (as Paul's admonitions to the Christians in Corinth make clear), but there were clear expectations that discipleship had economic consequences. The social programs of the churches provided for large numbers of people, including many nonmembers. Like the Anabaptists centuries later, the early Christians had no access to political power and could not effect structural changes in society; but their churches modeled counter-cultural approaches to the use of possessions and property, and insisted on regarding economics as a spiritual issue.

A new scenario opened up, of course, in the fourth century when the emperor embraced Christianity. Now the churches had access to the political process and could work for economic justice and social transformation. But the churches were also now recipients of imperial largesse and increasingly populated by wealthier citizens, who were not at all inclined to link spirituality with economics, disburse their possessions, or challenge the system that ensured their wealth and social status. The churches encouraged charitable giving to meet the needs of the poor and developed various institutions to care for the victims of the system they now helped to sustain, but there was no longer any appetite to challenge the system itself.

Over the centuries, not only did the church become an extremely wealthy institution and a major landowner, but the introduction of tithing (a Christendom innovation) resulted in misery and economic hardship for the poorest members of society.[3] The peasants' revolt in the sixteenth century was a desperate protest, inspired by the gospel, against economic abuses in the churches as well as in the rest of society. The reformers also were outraged by the corrupt and unspiritual economic practices of church authorities (including the sale of indulgences), but they were wedded to the Christendom system and too dependent on the support of the authorities to pursue economic justice across society.

It was left to the Anabaptists, following in the wake of earlier dissenting movements, to develop a more trenchant critique of the economic assumptions that undergirded society. With less invested in the status quo and with a deep suspicion of the Christendom system, they took their lead from the teaching of Jesus and the example of the early churches.

This critique was so troubling to the authorities that some issued official warnings against it. The thirty-eighth article of the Church of England's *Thirty-Nine Articles of Religion* (1571) reads, "The riches and goods of Christians are not common, as touching the right, title, and possession of the same, as certain Anabaptists do falsely boast." Good Anglicans, this article insists, should be generous in sharing their resources, but they should not be misled by radical and socially disruptive Anabaptist notions, which undermined the foundational principle of private ownership.

COMMON OWNERSHIP AND MUTUAL AID

Did Anabaptists teach and practice common ownership of possessions? Certainly not in England, where there were very few Anabaptists at all in the sixteenth century but where fear of this movement apparently required its naming and shaming. Nor did Anabaptists in most other parts of Europe. But the Moravian Hutterites developed common-purse communities in which all but a few personal belongings were held in common and the notion of private property was regarded as contrary to the gospel. Although necessity may have played some part in this policy, as refugee communities supported each other on their journey away from persecution and in the early stages of settling on new lands, there were underlying theological arguments, and the Hutterites based their practice on biblical texts (especially Acts 2–4).

A more notorious example of common ownership was the Anabaptist city of Münster, in which it was reported that wives were held in common as well as property. The siege and capture of this city and the massacre of its inhabitants may have eradicated this particular outbreak of communalism, but the authorities were determined to suppress a movement capable of such an outrage.[4] Münster offered church and civic leaders across Europe the evidence they needed to declare Anabaptism misguided and dangerous. It was Münster, rather than Moravia, that prompted the thirty-eighth article's denunciation of Anabaptists.

However, the majority of Anabaptists did not practice "community of goods" but "mutual aid." This meant that they continued to own property and possessions, but made these available freely and gladly as they encountered others in need. It is this approach to economics that has characterized most Anabaptist communities. Hutterite communities persist, and other common-purse communities (such as the Bruderhofs) have emerged, inspired by or connecting with the Anabaptist tradition.[5] But most Anabaptists today are exploring the implications of mutual aid rather than community of goods.

How does the practice of mutual aid differ from the charitable giving advocated by the thirty-eighth article as an alternative to Anabaptist economics? The sixth core conviction identifies some of the implications.

First, economics and spirituality are connected for reasons of justice rather than charity. The backdrop to this conviction is a global economic order that is profoundly unjust, in which vast numbers are kept impoverished within a system that benefits and protects the powerful few. Charitable giving to offset some of the worst effects of this unjust system is laudable, but this can appease our consciences and distract us from working toward a more just world. The Anabaptist commitment to mutual aid recognizes the prior claim of others in need to what we possess—as a matter of justice, rather than charity.

This picks up the disturbing New Testament challenge: "How does God's love abide in anyone who has the world's goods and sees a brother or sister in need and yet refuses help?" (1 John 3:17). The apostle John insists that the quality (indeed the validity) of our spiritual life, our experience of God, is integrally related to our economic discipleship. We may struggle to work out the practical application of this principle in a world of overwhelming needs, but we will be guided by a concern for justice and a vision of a different world.

Second, the practice of mutual aid confronts the pervasive individualism of contemporary western societies. Nowhere is individualism more apparent than in the economic sphere. Our property is private. Our possessions belong to us and are jealously safeguarded. Our homes are our castles, well-defended against any intruders. Most of us do not disclose the level of our salaries or savings to others, nor do we invite others to help us think through where we might live, what standard of living is appropriate, or how we might utilize our resources. It is quite unnecessary for our churches to conform to these cultural norms. If our churches are not institutions but communities, and if we recognize our need for each other's help in discerning and resisting the economic pressures of our culture, mutual aid will consist not just in sharing resources but also in working out *together* how to be disciples of Jesus in the area of economics. This economic practice will impact our spirituality.

Third, the practice of charitable giving does not generally raise questions about what we retain or about our lifestyle. Consequently, we are prone to succumb to consumerism and find it hard to untangle the confusion of needs and wants promulgated by the advertising industry. Anabaptist communities have often been associated with two counter-cultural values: simplicity and contentment. These values have implications for both economics and spirituality. Historically, Anabaptists have also questioned the charging of interest on loans, the accumulation of wealth, even through legitimate occupations, and the propriety of making money without producing anything of actual value ("merchandising"). These concerns represent fundamental challenges to contemporary economic assumptions and practices. A spirituality of simplicity and contentment (a spirituality of "enough") may be counter-cultural but also liberating.

Fourth, mutual aid implies reciprocity and relationship. The sharing of resources is not all in one direction, which so often leads to dependency and disempowerment. Nor does this take place at arm's length or in impersonal ways. Familiar practices within the Anabaptist tradition include "barn raising" among the Amish, as neighbors rally around to help those in need, aware that one of the helpers might be the next to need help; and the readiness of Mennonites to go to disaster zones to help personally in addition to sending donations.

Anabaptists have not always embraced these principles or practiced them consistently and creatively. Nor are these principles unique to the Anabaptist tradition. But we have learned from this tradition and are "committed to finding ways" of working out the economic dimensions of discipleship in contemporary culture and exploring further the deep connection between economics and spirituality. What has economic discipleship meant in practice for British and Irish Anabaptists?

- Exploring alternatives to mortgages to enable members of a church community to purchase houses.

- Challenging the widespread practice of tithing as a distortion of biblical teaching, capitulation to individualism, and failure to address issues of inequality.

- Deploying in poor urban communities church-planting teams committed to mutual support of their members, openness about their finances, and "uncluttered lives."

- Investigating the implications of the biblical principles of Jubilee and *koinonia* for church and society.[6]

- Inviting trusted friends to provide accountability in the area of personal finance to counter the impact of individualism and consumerism.

- An unusually strong emphasis on hospitality and sharing meals together in order to build community.

- Active involvement in initiatives and organizations working for greater justice at local and global levels (such as Jubilee 2000 and Make Poverty History).

- Prophetic actions, such as the Day of Action in Westminster, England, inspired by the book of Ezekiel and organized by Speak in 2006, to highlight issues of injustice.

The testimony of the early Anabaptists—a testimony echoed by Christians in many other traditions—is that wealth and security can hinder personal and corporate spiritual growth. Some Anabaptist prisoners reported that it was much easier to pray in prison than outside. Fewer distractions, fear of torture and execution, hunger and thirst resulted in fervent and desperate prayer and a sense of the nearness of God. Some Anabaptist writers questioned whether preachers paid by the state and living in comfort could truly discern and preach the word of God. The Anabaptist tradition might ask whether lower living standards and reduced security could be at least as conducive to genuine spiritual growth as listening to sermons, participating in worship services, or visiting retreat centers.

On one aspect of this core conviction, the historic Anabaptist tradition seems to have little to contribute. Caring for creation was not an issue that Anabaptists, or other Christians in the sixteenth century, addressed. But most Anabaptists through the centuries have lived close to the land, and in many Anabaptist communities today, the link between spirituality and responsibility for the earth is strong. Our experience has been that many Christians who are concerned about creation care find the Anabaptist tradition congenial and that Anabaptist values have encouraged others to think seriously about this issue. Until very recently, the coordinator of the Eco-Congregation program[7] and the chief executive of a leading environmental agency were both members of the Anabaptist Network's steering group.

Two central Anabaptist convictions underscore the significance of caring for creation, even if these were not until recently interpreted in this way. The first is the emphasis on the humanity of Jesus within the Anabaptist tradition. The incarnation means that "matter matters." The second is the commitment to peace, to which we turn next. If the mission of God is reconciliation, this applies not only to human beings but to the whole of creation.

> Peace is at the heart of the gospel. As followers of Jesus in a divided and violent world, we are committed to finding nonviolent alternatives and to learning how to make peace between individuals, within and among churches, in society, and between nations.

Anabaptism belongs to the so-called "historic peace church" tradition. Peace churches are not just opposed to violence (and especially lethal violence) in all its forms, but believe that peace is fundamental to the gospel, rather than an incidental, optional, or peripheral issue. A commitment to peace has been characteristic of Anabaptist churches through the centuries.

ANABAPTISTS AND NONVIOLENCE

If their economic practices (common-purse communities and mutual aid) disturbed their contemporaries, the refusal of most Anabaptists to take up arms was equally worrying. All European citizens were expected to defend their homes and families, obey the summons to war, and repel the Turks or any other invaders. Pacifism was not an intellectual option that might be adopted without consequences: those who refused to take up arms were viewed as cowards and traitors.

Although pacifist convictions were present from the beginning of the movement, not all first-generation Anabaptists embraced these. Some were known as "sword bearers" rather than "staff bearers" and were prepared to fight in certain circumstances. Most adhered to strict separation between church and state and regarded civic offices as incompatible with Christian discipleship, not least because such offices might involve authorizing the use of violence, including capital punishment. But some thought it possible, though difficult, for true Christians to be magistrates.

By the middle of the sixteenth century, however, pacifism was well established as a core conviction of the Anabaptist tradition. Biblical interpretation and theological arguments undergirded this position, which all members of Anabaptist churches were expected to endorse. Although today principled pacifism is often respected, in the past (especially in times of war) Anabaptists were castigated and punished for their unwillingness to fight. Members of Anabaptist churches, succumbing to social pressure or dissenting from their tradition, have sometimes decided to join up. And some Anabaptist churches today worry that their commitment to peace might be too much of a disincentive for others to join them. But most Anabaptists have continued to espouse and practice pacifism.

Anabaptists have also been deeply opposed to any form of religious coercion. Their own experiences of marginalization, discrimination, and persecution have made them sensitive to other minorities. Early Anabaptists championed the cause of religious liberty for all—not just for different varieties of Christians, but for Jews and Muslims too. But unlike those who conclude that advocating religious liberty is incompatible with evangelism, sixteenth-century Anabaptists were passionate evangelists. While not all contemporary Anabaptists have been able to hold together these dimensions of mission, some have recently been exploring the potential of peaceful witness for relationships with Muslims, in particular, and for the mission of the church in a religiously plural and divided world.[8]

The resilience of this commitment to peace as an essential dimension of the gospel distinguishes the Anabaptist tradition from several other movements that embraced what is often known as the "peace witness" in their early years but moved away from this commitment in subsequent generations. Examples of this tendency include the Disciples of Christ, the Plymouth Brethren, and the Assemblies of God. First-generation communities, it seems, as they engage afresh with New Testament teaching, often recognize that "peace is at the heart of the gospel," but only occasionally does this conviction persist.

This is perhaps not surprising in light of the teaching and practice of mainline churches. For many centuries the churches have endorsed lethal violence, blessed the weapons of war, prayed for military success, celebrated victories in acts of worship, and deployed missionaries under the protection of conquering armies. So closely have the churches been identified with imperial or national interests that they have struggled to distinguish between political and spiritual advances or to challenge the ubiquity of warfare. There have, of course, been courageous individual voices raised in protest, but the dominant voices in the western church have endorsed and justified the use of violence.

PEACE, WAR, AND CHRISTENDOM

The peace witness of the Anabaptist tradition reaches back to the teaching and practice of the early churches. Before Constantine's conversion, attitudes toward war and peace were very different. Until about 170, the church was predominantly pacifist in teaching and practice. In many ways this was understandable: there was no universal conscription, few soldiers were converted, and the church was a marginal community on the fringes of mainstream society. There were no incentives to go to war. However, the evidence suggests that there were more fundamental objections. Love and killing were regarded as incompatible, and the church's self-identity was a culture of peace, patterned on the example and teaching of Jesus.[9]

Between 170 and 313, there were changes. As the church grew numerically and became more socially acceptable, attracting a wider range of converts, including some from the military, many tried to be both good Christians and good Romans. Sensitive to criticism from pagan contemporaries that they benefited from an empire they refused to defend, some Christians began to join the army. But this provoked strong resistance from church leaders, and some who enlisted refused to kill, sometimes being executed for this stance.

Constantine's conversion resulted in massive and rapid changes in the relationship between the church and warfare. The cross became a military emblem. Large numbers of soldiers joined the burgeoning churches, and other Christians enlisted in the imperial army that was now charged with defending an increasingly "Christian" society. Church leaders authorized killing in war and threatened with excommunication any soldier who dared to throw down his arms. A little over a century later, in 416, only professing Christians were allowed to join the army. The church had made peace with war.

During the Christendom era, the partnership between church and state required a fresh approach to the question of war and peace. Pacifism seemed totally unrealistic in this new context. But the peace witness of the first three hundred years could not simply be swept away. So how was the church to justify the participation of its members in warfare?

The solution was provided by the most influential theologian of the early Christendom era, Augustine, bishop of Hippo. Drawing on pagan philosophical ideas and adapting these to suit a Christian audience, Augustine advocated the doctrine known subsequently as "just war." This doctrine offered the church guidelines, criteria to apply to ascertain whether or not a given conflict was justified. It in no way glorified warfare but insisted that war was sometimes better than allowing injustice to persist or invaders to triumph.

This doctrine had no basis in Scripture or the teaching of the early churches (Augustine himself did not seem entirely at ease as he explained away troublesome New Testament passages). But it was gratefully accepted by church leaders trying to come to terms with their new social context and attempting to woo the resistant pagan aristocracy. And this has been the dominant approach within the church ever since. Participation in warfare was justifiable, this doctrine concluded, if the cause was just, the intention was good, there was a reasonable expectation of success, the means were appropriate, all other options had been exhausted, and war was declared and fought by a legitimate authority.

Some Christians continue to defend this doctrine as a helpful and realistic approach to the challenges and ambiguities of a fallen world. The guidelines are actually very stringent, for every condition has to be satisfied before a war can be justified. If applied rigorously, almost all wars in history would have been judged unjust. But no representative church body has *ever* pronounced a war declared or fought by the nation in which it was situated to be unjust. Discovering this, and recognizing that the ancient criteria are extraordinarily difficult to apply to contemporary scenarios, increasing numbers of Christians today are reluctant to affirm this approach.

Even fewer have any sympathy with the other main approach to war in the Christendom era—the crusade, or "holy war," in which the normal criteria could be set aside in cases where the enemy was obviously evil and the cause of the gospel was at stake. Arguably, this approach has a stronger biblical foundation (at least in the Old Testament) than the just war doctrine, but it has little else to commend it.

LEARNING TO MAKE PEACE

Not surprisingly, then, many Christians today are drawn to the position advocated by the historic peace churches, including the Anabaptists. Some are still concerned that injustice may flourish until forceful action is taken and are not yet fully persuaded that nonviolent intervention is as effective as its proponents claim. Others still confuse pacifism with "passivism." But the horrors of modern warfare, the seemingly endless cycle of violence that followed the "war to end all wars" early in the twentieth century, and increasing skepticism about the reasons politicians give for going to war, all conspire to challenge long-held assumptions and guidelines. One of the most malign legacies of Christendom may be under threat.

In societies where people of many faiths and none are now reluctant to endorse the use of lethal violence for supposedly "just" causes, the Anabaptist tradition offers an alternative perspective. This is not derived from the liberal values of secular humanism (which have espoused another from of pacifism), but from the example and teaching of Jesus. Nor is Anabaptist pacifism an instance of the church capitulating to a cultural trend but a deeply rooted conviction, tested in the fires of persecution, which has endured for five centuries.

It is the peace witness of the Anabaptist tradition that has attracted Christians from many other traditions. Not all are convinced pacifists, but most are convinced that "peace is at the heart of the gospel," that Christians are called to pursue peace as well as justice, and that we need to take with utmost seriousness Jesus' insistence that we love our enemies. This final core conviction examines what Anabaptists today mean by peace and commits us to pursuing peace in all areas of life.

Peace, of course, is multifaceted, especially if we have in view the remarkably rich Old Testament concept of *shalom*. The biblical vision of universal restoration (Acts 3:21) includes peace between God and humanity; enemies reconciled; disintegrated personalities healed; weapons of war decommissioned and transformed into agricultural implements; injustice and oppression removed; communities flourishing; creation liberated from bondage; and the abolition of sickness and death. Peace is at the heart of the gospel because the mission of God is to bring peace to the whole of creation.

The Anabaptist commitment to nonviolence, then, is not founded on naïve expectations that people can be persuaded to be nice to each other. We realize that we are followers of Jesus in a divided and violent world, and we are utterly realistic about the evil that lurks in the hearts of our fellow human beings—and in our own hearts—and spills out in acts of terrible violence. But we are followers of Jesus, the Prince of Peace, and we choose to believe that his way of nonviolent love is ultimately more realistic than embracing violence. Whether or not nonviolent alternatives are effective in the short term, or even the medium term, peace churches are signs of the coming kingdom of God. We choose to align ourselves with the future to which God is leading history.[10]

While Anabaptists have consistently opposed the use of lethal violence, especially in war, but also in the criminal justice system, they have often struggled to respond convincingly to two interrelated challenges. If violent means are renounced, doesn't this mean that in many situations injustice will go unchecked? And are nonviolent alternatives effective within history?

Anabaptists through the centuries have been guilty of passivity in the face of injustice, of disengagement from society, of confusing "nonviolence" with "nonresistance," of failing to move beyond opposition to war toward finding alternatives, of irresponsible idealism and otherworldly forms of spirituality. But many Anabaptists today, as this core conviction suggests, are committed to learning how to make peace and finding nonviolent alternatives. These are proactive commitments and move us away from "passivism" and disengagement.

Indeed, Anabaptists have been at the forefront of initiatives to develop creative alternatives to conventional approaches. For example,

- Christian Peacemaker Teams are deployed in conflict zones to support those who are working nonviolently for peace and justice in their communities.[11] Two members of the Anabaptist Network steering group were heading off to join a team in Latin America just as this book was being completed.

- Conflict transformation initiatives train individuals and communities in the processes and practices that can enable them to handle conflict creatively and experience this as transformative rather than destructive. The Bridge Builders program based at the London Mennonite Centre has developed considerable expertise in this area.[12]

- "Peacemakers" is a children's holiday club program developed by members of the Anabaptist Network and pioneered in a multicultural, inner-city community. It has helped children from different faith communities to learn about reconciliation and peacemaking and has recently been adopted by local schools.

- Victim-offender reconciliation programs and other restorative-justice practices offer constructive alternatives to retributive and anonymous approaches to crime and punishment.[13] Members of the Anabaptist Association of Australia and New Zealand have been deeply involved in these developments.

Such "peace initiatives" are sometimes criticized for their well-intentioned but dangerous naïveté. Those who pioneer these alternatives to conventional wisdom acknowledge that mistakes have been made and that their methods are still developing. The long-term effectiveness of these relatively recent initiatives is inevitably as yet unproven. But some of these programs have been operating long enough for their potential to be recognized and their principles embraced by others.[14] Poorly resourced by comparison with military and retributive systems, these peacemaking initiatives are beginning to bear fruit.

There is, in fact, mounting evidence that nonviolent resistance can catalyze political and social transformation, and that restorative and relational approaches to crime and injustice offer more to victims and wider society. And there is abundant evidence (albeit ignored by those who are locked into conventional ways of thinking and reacting) that retributive and violent methods are ineffective and breed further violence and criminality. Maybe it is time to give peacemaking initiatives a chance to demonstrate what they can achieve.

Embracing alternatives to conventional wisdom will require courage, imagination, and persistence. For deeply embedded in our culture is what Walter Wink calls "the myth of redemptive violence."[15] This myth was propagated throughout the Christendom era and given powerful theological underpinning. The demise of Christendom is an opportunity to challenge this myth and the theology it is built on, and to develop creative alternatives that offer hope in a divided world—a world that is weary of violence and might be ready to consider different ways of resolving conflict.

Because conflict is multifaceted, so must our responses be as we explore strategies for making peace "between individuals, within and among churches, in society, and between nations." While we cannot wait until our churches have learned how to engage creatively with conflict, putting our own houses in order is essential if we are to address conflict in other contexts with integrity. Anabaptists through the centuries have experienced not a little internal conflict, sometimes leading to division and rancor, so the contribution of the Anabaptist tradition to contemporary peacemaking initiatives will include salutary warnings as well as encouraging examples. But Anabaptists, unlike Christians in most other traditions, have not killed those they have fallen out with. The Anabaptist tradition is an unusually potent resource for would-be peacemakers, pointing us back to the life and teaching of Jesus and offering historical examples of nonviolent resistance, loving our enemies, and the struggle to be faithful.

Dirk Willems is an iconic figure in the Anabaptist tradition, a member of an underground church in Asperen in the Netherlands in the second half of the sixteenth century. Arrested and imprisoned, he managed somehow to escape. Fleeing across a frozen canal, he heard the ice give way behind him and turned back to rescue from the icy water a bailiff who had been pursuing him. This compassionate act cost Dirk his life: he was promptly rearrested and soon afterward burned at the stake. As Anabaptists have reflected on this story and asked why Dirk turned back, many have concluded that this instinctive response (there was no time for careful analysis of the pros and cons) was the result of being nurtured by a community in which enemy-loving was regarded as normative for disciples of Jesus.

Perhaps, then, one of the first steps in "learning how to make peace" and "finding nonviolent alternatives" is to develop "peace churches" that nurture unconventional reflexes and free our imaginations to explore creative possibilities. I am sometimes asked how I would act if someone broke into my house and threatened someone I loved (a familiar challenge to pacifists). My response is that there are some things I know I would not do. I would not shoot them, because I have no gun. But I don't know how I would respond. My hope is that I have been "learning how to make peace" through my engagement with Scripture and the Anabaptist tradition and that I would find a creative and nonviolent way to respond.

Maybe the way forward is to take some small steps that might inspire larger and more costly steps. On my office wall is a poster advocating "a modest proposal for peace." M. R. Zigler, a Church of the Brethren peacemaker, and John Stoner, a Mennonite leader, proposed in 1984, "Let the Christians of the world agree that they will not kill each other." Responses to this proposal have been interesting, as I have tested it out in many contexts. Quite often it takes a while for people to appreciate its disturbing significance and the way its implications ripple out. Most agree that they should not kill other members of their own congregation. They then extend this to other congregations in their own denomination and beyond it. But what about Christians from other nations in war zones or Christian combatants in opposing armies? And how do we know who are the Christian soldiers or civilians in war zones? And why should we give preferential treatment to Christians? Gradually the challenge of this "modest proposal" dawns on us.

CONCLUSION

The issues of provision and protection are of fundamental importance in all societies. Because they impact some of our most basic needs, debates about these issues provoke strong reactions, especially when the dominant norms and assumptions are challenged. But such debates may be both timely and essential in societies where long-held beliefs about the efficacy of violence (or the threat of violence) and the self-regulating capacity of market forces in an economy based on private property and self-interest are no longer self-evidently true. Perhaps, after all, a culture built on military consumerism is unstable. And perhaps the disintegration of Christendom offers western Christians an opportunity to revisit these issues and disavow our collusion with wealth and violence.

If so, the Anabaptist tradition offers insights and resources that many are finding helpful. But it is worth emphasizing again, as we conclude our investigation of these seven core convictions, that the Anabaptist tradition is only one of many traditions on which we will need to draw as we discover what it means to be followers of Jesus in a changing world. And the Anabaptist tradition has flaws and weaknesses, so those who identify primarily with this tradition need to be realistic about these and grateful for insights from other traditions.

In the final chapter, in the spirit of *The Naked Anabaptist*, we will expose some of the blemishes and imperfections of Anabaptism, but the next chapter offers an overview of the history of the movement. Some readers may prefer to skip this historical chapter, but others may find this a helpful framework in which to place various references in the past four chapters to Anabaptist practices through the centuries.

7

The Original Anabaptists

THE PREVIOUS four chapters have expounded the convictions and commitments of Christians who identify with the Anabaptist tradition today. These represent an attempt by followers of Jesus in Britain and Ireland at the beginning of the twenty-first century to interpret the Anabaptist vision, to distill its essence, to clothe "the naked Anabaptist" for this context. But is this interpretation authentic? How does it square with the interpretations of others who have shaped their lives and communities in light of the Anabaptist vision over the past five centuries? And how faithfully does it reflect the vision and values of the original Anabaptists?

We have certainly been alert to the danger of reinterpreting the Anabaptist vision so that it means whatever we want it to mean, though this is no guarantee that we have avoided that trap. We have taken some precautionary measures. We have maintained links with Mennonite churches in Europe and North America, and we have from time to time visited a Hutterite-related community in England. These historic expressions of Anabaptism can help us discern where we have moved away from or distorted the original vision. And we take care to retell the stories of the sixteenth-century Anabaptists, so that we can test our convictions and priorities against theirs.

Mennonite, Hutterite, and Amish communities have interpreted Anabaptism in different ways, holding on to some practices through the centuries and adapting others to changing circumstances. We do not feel obliged to copy everything they do or to agree with all their interpretations, but we value their experience and want to learn from it. Without these conversation partners, neo-Anabaptists will be prone to idealizing and romanticizing the Anabaptist tradition. The final section of this chapter pays tribute to these communities and indicates some of the ways they inspire, challenge, and disturb us.

However, it is important first to look back to the original Anabaptists, from whom all these communities, and those who choose to identify with the Anabaptist tradition, take their bearings. Who were they? What did they believe? What were their hopes and dreams? Why were they persecuted? Why did they persist in the face of opposition and suffering? What is their legacy to future generations?

EMERGING ANABAPTISTS

The Anabaptist "movement" in the first half of the sixteenth century gradually coalesced out of several independent initiatives. Local factors influenced their shape and priorities, so what emerged was by no means uniform. But as news of these developments spread, and as representatives of these groups visited each other, it became clear to them—and to the increasingly worried authorities—that beneath their regional variations there was an underlying unity and many shared convictions.

The shared convictions can be explained in different ways: as a sign that these initiatives were inspired by the Holy Spirit; as a consequence of people reading the Bible without proper supervision and rejecting traditional church practices that they could not find there; as responses to the social, economic, and political turmoil that was sweeping across Europe; or, so their opponents insisted, as evidence that they were all deluded and deceived.

There are certainly striking similarities between these convictions and those of dissident groups in previous centuries who had also dared to read the Bible without submitting to official interpretations. Throughout the Christendom era, despite the determined efforts of the authorities to eradicate them, these "heretical" ideas surfaced repeatedly. Previously, the dissidents' hand-copied literature had been relatively easy to suppress, but Anabaptists had the new technology of printing at their disposal. Underground presses churned out their tracts, spreading their views, linking disparate groups together and frustrating attempts to silence them.

The significance of the Anabaptist movement is not limited to the sixteenth-century story: the Anabaptists were heirs to many silenced and persecuted Christians in earlier centuries who yearned for the recovery of authentic discipleship.[1] But we do need also to understand Anabaptism in its immediate context. Europe was in the throes of major cultural changes that were disrupting the political, economic, social, and religious arrangements that had persisted for several centuries.

- Medieval feudalism was giving way to capitalism, and a new urban middle class was growing in influence and threatening traditional social power structures.

- Nationalism was becoming an unstoppable force, as hundreds of principalities and several free cities vied for authority with the old Holy Roman Empire.

- These economic and political changes were causing serious hardship among the peasants, provoking a widespread but short-lived revolt in the mid-1520s.

- Attempts to reform the massively wealthy, bureaucratic, and corrupt institutional church had been unsuccessful, but demands for reform were insistent.

Anabaptism emerged on the back of two very different attempts to bring transformation to church and society.

In 1517, Martin Luther composed and distributed ninety-five theses urging the removal of abuses and wholesale reformation of the Catholic Church. As well as allegedly nailing these to the door of the Castle Church in Wittenberg, Germany, Luther used the new technology of printing to copy these theses and send them out across Europe. Obtaining the support and protection of the Elector of Saxony, Luther was able to resist all attempts by the pope and the emperor to call him to account.

This was the start of the Protestant Reformation that spread rapidly across Europe and resulted in the disintegration of Christendom. This was not Luther's intention. He wanted to reform the church, not to divide it. But the Catholic Church could not respond quickly or creatively enough to prevent this: from the 1560s the so-called "counter-Reformation" regained the initiative in some areas, but Europe was by then divided into Protestant and Catholic territories.

As enthusiasm for reform spread in the early 1520s, peasant leaders began to advocate for economic and social reforms alongside the reform of the church. As with the Anabaptist movement later in the decade, the peasants' movement sprang up in several places and only gradually combined their resources in recognition of a shared agenda. The peasants presented demands to the authorities, based on the teachings of the New Testament, and began to engage in non-violent forms of civil disobedience.[2]

As the movement spread and local protests became regional, the authorities became increasingly concerned and took stronger action. The peasants were waiting for Luther and his colleagues to declare their support but, to their dismay, Luther instead issued a harsh treatise, *Against the Robbing and Murdering Hordes of Peasants*, in which he urged the authorities to crush the movement. One or two reformers who had fallen out with Luther—most notoriously Thomas Müntzer—joined the peasants, but the movement was annihilated at the Battle of Frankenhausen in 1525.

Some early Anabaptist leaders were involved in the reform movement that Luther started; not least were several colleagues of Ulrich Zwingli in Zürich. They became frustrated with the slow progress there and withdrew their support in order to pursue a more radical vision. Others were caught up in the peasants' movement, including escapees from the disaster at Frankenhausen. They recognized that there was no prospect of implementing the political and economic changes they had fought for and decided to pursue their vision of a just and harmonious community in other ways. Anabaptism emerged as scattered groups seeking alternative strategies for reform coalesced, offering fresh hope to men and women who had been disappointed by other attempts to reform church and society.

ANABAPTISTS IN SWITZERLAND

On the evening of January 21, 1525, less than eight years after the start of the Protestant Reformation, a small group of Christians were meeting secretly in a house in Zürich to talk and pray together. They had been enthusiastic followers of Zwingli, minister of the Grossmünster (the main church in the city), who was attempting to reform both the church and the city of Zürich. They had studied the Bible with him, listened attentively to his sermons, shared his convictions, and supported his reform program. But they were now deeply troubled by his apparent reluctance to follow through on what he had been preaching and to implement what they regarded as clear biblical teaching on a number of issues, including the baptism of believers rather than infants.

Zwingli was committed to a citywide reformation, which needed the support of the city council. It was his task, he believed, to advocate reformation on the basis of Scripture, but the council must decide how and when to implement these reforms. Zwingli refused to press too hard or move too quickly and risk alienating the civic authorities. But some of his followers were not prepared to move at such a slow pace and were not convinced that reform needed to be authorized by the authorities. Over the previous two years they had agitated for faster and more radical action. The city council had organized public debates to examine the arguments and had, not surprisingly, backed the more gradual program proposed by Zwingli.

But the radicals were not satisfied and were becoming convinced that they faced a choice between obeying the city council and obeying God. The meeting on January 21 was the culmination of many months of Bible study and discussion, during which the issue of baptism had come to the fore. Some of those present had already risked punishment by refusing to baptize their children, but they were now considering a more radical step.

The Bible, they believed, taught that believers should be baptized. They had all been baptized as infants, but they now regarded this as unbiblical and ineffectual. So they wanted to be baptized as believers, as men and women who were freely choosing to become followers of Jesus and who had counted the cost of discipleship. This more radical step would be very costly indeed. They might discount their baptism as infants but, in the eyes of the authorities, what they were considering was "rebaptism"—an offense punishable by death.

Why did rebaptism attract such a harsh penalty? Because it

struck at the heart of the Christendom system, challenged the idea of a territorial church to which all citizens belonged from birth, and threatened to divide the community. It was treasonous as well as unorthodox. Legislation enacted many centuries earlier to counter the threat of the Donatist movement in North Africa could be used against any who dared to be rebaptized. Claiming that this was baptism, not *re*baptism, would be no defense. So this was not a step to be taken lightly.

Nevertheless, after a time of heart searching and fervent prayer, "George [Blaurock] stood up and besought Conrad Grebel for God's sake to baptize him with the true Christian baptism upon his faith and knowledge. And when he knelt down with such a request and desire, Conrad baptized him." In these famous words, *The Chronicle of the Hutterian Brethren* reported the first recorded instance of believers baptism in the Reformation era and the start of what soon became known as the Anabaptist ("rebaptizing") movement.

George Blaurock and Conrad Grebel were two of the early leaders of the Swiss Brethren (as the Anabaptists who originated in Zürich are often known). Grebel was the son of a city councillor who had been a member of Zwingli's inner circle; Blaurock was a former Catholic priest. Other significant figures were Felix Manz, a biblical scholar and another of Zwingli's disciples, who was the first Anabaptist to be executed by the city authorities—drowned in the Limmat river; Simon Stumpf, pastor in the village of Höngg, who incited his congregation to smash "idolatrous" images and statues in the parish church; Margaret Hottinger, a charismatic evangelist from Zollikon, imprisoned and eventually drowned for her faith; and Wilhelm Reublin, pastor in the nearby town of Witikon, who urged his parishioners to stop paying the tithe.

The execution of Manz in January 1527, less than two years after the first baptisms, was intended to demonstrate that the city authorities would not tolerate this radical movement. Persecution followed the Anabaptists wherever they went. But the movement was already spreading beyond the city and taking root in the countryside, partly because the Zürich group was determined to evangelize elsewhere and partly because Anabaptists deported from the city found themselves in the neighboring towns and villages. In

Zollikon, just outside Zürich, many were baptized amid scenes of deep conviction and spiritual revival, and Anabaptism flourished there despite arrests and imprisonment.

Within months the movement had spread east to St. Gall and Appenzell, west to Basel and Bern, and north to Hallau, Schaffhausen, and (across the border in Catholic territory under the control of the Austrian Hapsburgs) Waldshut. Already Waldshut was moving in the direction of reform under the leadership of Balthasar Hubmaier, a former Catholic priest, who had participated in the public debates in Zürich and who would become the foremost theologian in the Anabaptist movement. The city was also being drawn into the peasants' movement, supporting the peasants with supplies and troops. Grebel and Wilhelm Reublin visited Hubmaier several times and, on Easter Sunday 1525, Reublin baptized him. Hubmaier then baptized three hundred others and, before long, most of the citizens and many of the city councillors had been baptized, turning Waldshut, albeit briefly, into an "Anabaptist city."

There was popular support for Anabaptism also in Hallau, another city sympathetic to the peasants, where most of the citizens were baptized by Reublin and his colleague Johannes Brötli. Here, and elsewhere, the Anabaptist movement intersected with the peasants' movement, recognizing shared concerns and offering mutual support. Contrary to what many have suggested, Anabaptism in its earliest period was by no means separatist or withdrawn from society.

But, by the end of 1525, the peasants' movement had been destroyed and the authorities were determined to snuff out any further threats, including Anabaptism. The prospect of more "Anabaptist cities" now seemed remote. Hubmaier, in his writings and in his future ministry in Nicholsburg in Moravia, seems not to have given up on this dream, but most Anabaptists realized that, if they were to survive, their only course was to pursue their vision within separatist, underground communities.

In February 1527, representatives of the scattered Anabaptist communities gathered in the village of Schleitheim. Out of their conversation came the "Schleitheim Confession"—seven articles setting out the distinctive convictions of the Swiss Brethren.[3] Not surprisingly, in light of the circumstances, these articles are decidedly separatist and uncompromising in tone. They are also thoroughly pacifist. This confession would be the rallying point for most Swiss Anabaptists (although some, including Hubmaier, dissented from some of its statements). Its probable author was Michael Sattler, a former prior of a monastery near Freiburg, who had become an Anabaptist leader during 1526.

If it was dangerous being an Anabaptist, it was even more perilous being an Anabaptist leader. The authorities targeted the leaders, and few survived for long. Manz and Grebel were already dead (Grebel died in 1526). Sattler was tortured and burned at the stake in Rottenburg in May 1527. Hubmaier was imprisoned in Vienna, tortured, and burned alive in March 1528. Blaurock, who had been evangelizing and pastoring in the Tyrol, was executed there in 1529. There were no safe places. Catholic and Protestant authorities alike imprisoned, fined, tortured, and executed Anabaptists—Catholics usually burned them; Protestants beheaded or drowned them.[4]

Some Swiss Anabaptists survived by going underground, especially in remote rural and mountainous regions. A few congregations persist today, known as Swiss Mennonites. But most eventually emigrated in search of refuge. Many fled east into Moravia, where they joined Anabaptists fleeing from other parts of Europe, but some traveled north or west into Germany and the Netherlands, evangelizing as they went. One colorful figure from Germany who seems to have encountered Anabaptism through Swiss missionaries was Margaret Hellwart, who was repeatedly chained to her kitchen floor to prevent her from contaminating her neighbors with her Anabaptist views.[5]

In Germany and the Netherlands, emigrating Swiss Brethren encountered other Anabaptist communities, who were different from them and yet recognizably members of the same movement. But these territories offered no more than temporary respite, and the Swiss Brethren found freedom to practice their faith only when they eventually emigrated to Pennsylvania and other regions of North America. Most are now known as Mennonites, adopting the name given to Anabaptists in the Netherlands, although a split in the late seventeenth century resulted in a conservative faction taking the name "Amish" from their founder, Jakob Ammann.

ANABAPTISTS IN SOUTH GERMANY AND AUSTRIA

Anabaptist communities began to emerge in South Germany and Austria very soon after the first baptisms in Zürich and before the movement was widespread in Swiss towns and villages. Leaders of these communities were aware of the Swiss Brethren. Hans Denck, a key figure in South German Anabaptism, had visited Anabaptists in St. Gall before being baptized. He also met Balthasar Hubmaier in Augsburg, Germany, in 1525 and Michael Sattler in Strasbourg in 1526. But South German and Austrian Anabaptism was markedly different from Swiss Anabaptism in its origins and emphases.

Thomas Müntzer, mentioned above as a reformer whose views became progressively more radical and less acceptable to Martin Luther, questioned the legitimacy of infant baptism, but he did not take the further step of becoming an Anabaptist. Intrigued by what they were hearing about him, the Swiss Brethren exchanged letters with him, but he had little influence on Swiss Anabaptism.

Not so in relation to South German Anabaptism. Müntzer had assumed leadership within the peasants' movement, drafting documents and finally leading them into battle, before being captured and executed. His influence lived on through those of his followers who escaped from the battlefield and founded Anabaptist congregations, most notably Hans Hut and Melchior Rinck. From Müntzer they inherited a passionate concern for social justice, a deep and mystical spirituality, and a conviction that the end of history was near. This was a potent mix that resulted in a very different style of Anabaptism from the Swiss communities.

Denck contributed another strand to South German Anabaptism. Temperamentally quite different from the firebrands who were inspired by Müntzer, he nevertheless shared their interest in mysticism. Denck was a classical scholar who became a supporter of the reform movement and was appointed to a teaching post in Nuremburg, Germany. Although he may have encountered Müntzer there in 1524, Denck did not become involved in the peasants' movement, but his dubious associations resulted in him being identified as a radical and expelled from the city. After visiting Swiss cities where the Anabaptist movement was in evidence and being imprisoned for challenging the practice of infant baptism, he returned to German territory. At some point he was baptized, because he was an Anabaptist leader in Augsburg by the end of 1525.

Denck died of the plague in November 1527, but in his two years as an Anabaptist leader he helped to lay the foundations of the movement in South Germany. In May 1526 Denck baptized Hut, who would be its foremost evangelist. Later that year he debated with the reformer Martin Bucer in front of several hundred people in Strasbourg. Moving on to Worms, he and Rinck built an Anabaptist community in the city and succeeded in winning over two young Lutheran preachers.

In his final months, though, he appears to have become somewhat disillusioned, especially by divisions within the movement. His insistence that the "inner word" (spiritual experience) was more important than external ceremonies and precise dogmas, and his advocacy of love and acceptance, were unusual in this period of mutual antagonism between professing Christians.

Hut was an entirely different personality. A bookseller by profession, he traveled widely before and after encountering Müntzer. Expelled from Bibra for refusing to allow his child to be baptized, he became a confidant of Müntzer and was arrested near the site of the battle of Frankenhausen, but escaped punishment by claiming to have been selling books rather than fighting. Returning to Bibra, he engaged in rather inflammatory preaching, predicting divine punishment on unworthy clerics, and was expelled again.

After his baptism in Augsburg, Hut was on the road constantly, baptizing thousands and planting Anabaptist churches in major cities, towns, and villages across South Germany and Austria. Three significant converts were Leonhard Schiemer, Hans Schlaffer, and Ambrosius Spittelmaier, who helped to spread Anabaptism in Austria. But Hut's fiery ministry lasted less than eighteen months. Seized in Augsburg, he was tortured and died in prison in 1527 before he could be executed.

Hut, like Denck and Müntzer, drank deeply from the mystical tradition. Although South German and Austrian Anabaptism owed much to the radical wing of the Lutheran reform movement, it owed more to the medieval German mystics (Meister Eckhart, Johannes

Tauler, and the *Theologia Deutsch*).[6] This gave the movement a different flavor from the biblically oriented and sober Swiss Brethren—at times charismatic, at times quietist, emphasizing the importance of yielding to the will of God. Like Müntzer, but unlike Denck, Hut also drew heavily on the apocalyptic sections of the Bible. This not only lent urgency to his activities but also impacted his teaching, as he presented baptism as "sealing the elect" for the last days and looked forward to the punishment of the wicked (in which Anabaptists might play some part).

A third, but less well-known, founding father of this branch of Anabaptism was Melchior Rinck. A classical scholar from Hesse who became a Lutheran preacher, Rinck fought at Frankenhausen but escaped the carnage and was probably baptized by Denck in January 1527 before working with him in Worms. In 1528 he was in Hersfeld, where he presented articles at a theological debate that resulted in his expulsion from the area. Rinck refused to accept this expulsion and continued to travel around Hesse and Saxony, preaching and baptizing, until he was arrested and imprisoned in 1531. Unusually, thanks to the leniency of Margrave Philip of Hesse, Rinck was not executed but remained in prison for the rest of his life, adamantly maintaining his Anabaptist convictions.

Less is known of Rinck's theological and spiritual views than those of Hut or Denck. He was clearly influenced initially by both Denck and Müntzer, but what evidence there is suggests that he was less interested in mysticism, eschatology, and revolution. In fact, his teaching seems closer to that of the Swiss Brethren, focusing on the foundational issues of repentance, faith, baptism, and discipleship.

South German and Austrian Anabaptism lacked the cohesion of the Swiss Brethren. Like the Swiss, they suffered the loss of key leaders very early, but unlike the Swiss, they did not coalesce around a confession of any kind. Perhaps this was inevitable in light of the diverse convictions and personalities of Denck, Hut, and Rinck and the emphasis on inner realities rather than externals. Four groups evolved from these beginnings: one pursued Hut's apocalyptic vision; another imbibed Denck's mystical spirituality; a third combined these emphases; and a fourth turned in a more separatist direction.

The other main figure in this branch of the Anabaptist movement was Pilgram Marpeck, a former mayor and mining magis-
trate of Rattenberg, Austria, until 1528. Initially attracted to the
Lutherans, Marpeck was disappointed by the lack of discipleship in
their churches and became an Anabaptist. Moving to Strasbourg,
France, where he worked as an engineer, Marpeck assumed leadership of an Anabaptist community in the city until exiled in 1532.
After a period on the move, interacting with Swiss and Moravian
Anabaptists, he settled again in Augsburg and led an Anabaptist
community there until his death in 1556 (one of very few Anabaptist leaders to survive so long unmolested). Marpeck's social position meant that he needed to wrestle seriously with the question
of how far to engage with the power structures of his day without
compromising his Anabaptist principles.

The groups associated with Marpeck seem not to have survived,
but his significance for the movement lies elsewhere. Not only did
he write extensively, but he corresponded with Anabaptists in other
areas, and his writings reflect the intra-Anabaptist discussions that
were taking place during the first thirty years. His own position was
a mediating one, as he encouraged the more literalist Swiss and the
more mystical South German groups to learn from one another.
Contemporary Anabaptists often find Marpeck the most attractive
and accessible of first-generation leaders.[7]

Cities such as Strasbourg and Augsburg offered some freedom for
Anabaptist churches to meet and for Anabaptist ideas to be debated,
but the threat of persecution was never far away. As pressure from the
authorities increased, many South German and Austrian Anabaptists
looked to Moravia with its sympathetic landowners as a place of tolera-
tion, and waves of refugees made the journey there. Although Swiss
Brethren refugees joined them and Balthasar Hubmaier had been influential in setting up the early communities, it was South German and
Austrian Anabaptists who dominated the burgeoning Anabaptist communities in Moravia that would eventually be known as the Hutterites
(after an early leader, Jakob Hutter). This communitarian branch of the
movement offers an intriguing and challenging interpretation of the
Anabaptist tradition, to which we will shortly return.

ANABAPTISTS IN NORTH GERMANY AND THE NETHERLANDS

It is not entirely consonant with the Anabaptist tradition to focus solely on the leaders of the movement. Anabaptism spread through the faithful living and courageous testimony of thousands of "ordinary" believers, who accepted opposition and suffering as normal for those who would follow Jesus wholeheartedly. We know the names and stories of some of these through surviving court records. Others appear in the *Martyrs Mirror*, the huge collection of martyr stories that has reminded generations of Anabaptists of their origins and history.[8] Many others—craftsmen, villagers, itinerant church planters, local pastors, farmers, housewives, and merchants—are lost from view.

But the origins of Anabaptism in North Germany and the Netherlands can be traced to a single charismatic and enigmatic leader: Melchior Hoffman. A furrier from Schwäbisch Hall, Germany, his journey illustrates how those yearning for reformation might gradually become more and more radical in their views and activities.

Hoffman initially identified with the Lutheran movement and by 1523 was working as a lay preacher in Livonia, until he was expelled. After a meeting with Luther in Wittenberg in 1525, he moved to Dorpat, where his anti-clericalism and message of social justice made him popular with the poor, but caused him to fall out with his Lutheran colleagues. He went to Stockholm as a Lutheran missionary and again stirred up controversy before moving to Schleswig-Holstein in 1527. There he turned decisively away from Luther and branded his former colleagues false prophets. In 1529, his property was confiscated and he was expelled once more.

Moving to Strasbourg, he interacted with reformers, "spiritualists,"[9] and several varieties of Anabaptists, blending different elements into his own theology. He was baptized there but formed his own group rather than joining an existing congregation. In this group were a number of influential women recognized as having prophetic gifts, including Ursula Jost and Barbara Rebstock. But Hoffman's revolutionary and anticlerical views alarmed the authorities, and he fled to escape arrest.

During the next three years, Hoffman traveled widely, evangelizing and baptizing hundreds of people. It was in the Netherlands, where a fierce controversy was raging over the nature of communion, that Hoffman's teaching was received most enthusiastically. Large numbers were drawn to Melchiorite Anabaptism, which combined mystical, apocalyptic, revolutionary, and (to a lesser degree) biblicist emphases.[10] This provoked persecution and, after several deaths, Hoffman ordered the suspension of baptisms, and the movement went underground.

Hoffman was imprisoned in 1533, apparently allowing himself to be arrested in the belief this was necessary for the New Jerusalem to be established in Strasbourg. He spent the remainder of his life in prison, dying perhaps ten years later, still awaiting the events he had prophesied. His movement grew and spread across the Netherlands and in parts of North Germany, but Hoffman's imprisonment left it without adequate leadership. In the next two years, a disaster would occur, which authorities across Europe would seize on as demonstrating that Anabaptists were indeed dangerous subversives.

Jan Matthys, a Haarlem baker, assumed leadership of the movement in response to a supposed revelation, and sent out twelve apostles to evangelize and baptize. Among the places they visited was the German town of Münster, where their reception convinced Matthys that Hoffman had been right that the New Jerusalem was imminent, but wrong about its location: Münster, not Strasbourg, was the chosen site. A group of Anabaptists, many of them from the Netherlands, won the support of the local electorate and issued a call to Anabaptists everywhere to make their way to Münster and become citizens of the New Jerusalem. Thousands attempted to reach the city, although most were turned back by the authorities.

Münster was quickly surrounded by troops under the command of the local bishop. Two failed assaults were followed by a blockade to starve the town into submission. Matthys led a desperate breakout, believing that God would deliver him, but he was killed. He was succeeded by Jan van Leiden, a young tailor who set himself up as a Davidic king. With the support of Bernhard Rothmann, the main theologian of the Melchiorite movement, he instituted sweeping and violent reforms, using Old Testament legislation as his mandate, introduced polygamy, mandated capital punishment for minor offenses, and awaited the descent of the New Jerusalem. After a prolonged siege, Münster was finally captured and its inhabitants massacred.[11]

Münster was the greatest catastrophe of early Anabaptist history, resulting in increasing persecution across Europe, even in previously tolerant areas. Although few Anabaptists elsewhere endorsed their actions, those who subjected the city to a reign of terror cannot be detached from the Anabaptist story. They may have been extremists, caught up in an apocalyptic frenzy; their interpretation of Scripture may have been atypical and bizarre; and they may have resorted to violence in ways that were utterly at odds with the pacifist convictions of most Anabaptists. But they were Anabaptists. It is no more legitimate to exclude them from the story than to treat them, as generations of historians have done, as representative of the movement.

Anabaptism in North Germany and the Netherlands survived the fall of Münster, but the movement lost coherence, fragmenting into several communities that reacted in different ways to what had happened. Most renounced violence, although Jan van Batenburg led a small group that still believed the New Jerusalem was imminent and carried out sporadic acts of destruction to prepare the way for this.

The most significant leader during the next few years was David Joris, who urged pacifism and emphasized interior spirituality to the extent that external marks of Anabaptism were regarded as unimportant. Communities of his followers persisted for several decades, but Joris failed in his attempts to reunite the movement under his leadership, and he eventually left the area.

The future of Anabaptism in the Netherlands rested with those who had rejected Münster all along and maintained a pacifist position. The key leaders were Obbe and Dirk Philips, both of whom were baptized by Hoffman himself; an ex-Catholic priest, Menno Simons, from whom the Mennonites take their name; and later Leenaert Bouwens.[12]

Menno was baptized by Obbe Philips and joined the movement in 1536. The following year he was ordained as an elder. He spent the rest of his life traveling among scattered Anabaptist communities, teaching and pastoring them, and gradually welding them into a coherent movement. These communities struggled with various issues, not the least of which were questions about church discipline and the relationship between the "spirit" and the "letter," and the movement experienced damaging splits. But Menno's extensive writings and patient ministry enabled Dutch Anabaptism to survive and thrive. Despite being a wanted man, he repeatedly escaped capture and eventually died peacefully.

Obbe Philips soon left the movement, but Dirk exercised effective pastoral leadership for many years as Menno's colleague and also left a substantial body of writings. Bouwens, who was ordained by Menno in 1556, was a leading second-generation figure, traveling extensively across the region and baptizing (according to his own detailed account) more than ten thousand people in the second half of the sixteenth century.

North German and Dutch Anabaptists survived in many places, despite persecution. The area of Friesland in the north of the Netherlands was a place of refuge for many, but there were also vibrant communities in Amsterdam and elsewhere.[13] Indeed, Dutch Mennonites (also known as Doopsgezinde) entered a "golden age" in which they produced successful artists, doctors, businesspeople, government officials, scholars, and engineers (including the engineer who designed the huge dike around the inland sea). Although many of their churches are now struggling, Mennonites have maintained a presence in many areas of the Netherlands until the present day.

Anabaptism also flourished in Antwerp and other parts of Flanders until growing pressure led to mass emigration. Further north, Anabaptists spread along the Baltic coast, reaching Danzig, Prussia, and Poland. During the eighteenth century, many Mennonites moved even further east, settling in Ukraine and Russia, before eventually emigrating to Central, North, and South America.

AN EVOLVING MOVEMENT

The Swiss, South German/Austrian, and North German/Dutch branches of Anabaptism were not isolated from each other, as we have seen. There were significant theological and cultural differences between these expressions of Anabaptism, each of which represented responses to regional factors as well as the broader concern for refor-mation. But letters, visits, and conversations enabled the exchange of ideas and provoked passionate debates.

We have noted already interaction between Swiss and South Ger-man groups and between Melchior Hoffman and other Anabaptists in Strasbourg. There were many other places in which Anabaptists from different regions met during the first three decades. A poignant exam-ple was the "Martyrs' Synod" in 1527 in Augsburg (so called because many of those involved would become martyrs), where Swiss Brethren and South German Anabaptists explored various contentious issues together.

The flight of Anabaptists in various directions in search of refuge from persecution mixed up the different groups even further, especially in centers like Strasbourg, which offered a safe haven for a while to dif-ferent Anabaptist communities. In the 1550s, another round of discus-sions, this time between North German/Dutch and Swiss Anabaptists, took place in Strasbourg. Although these discussions did not bring about immediate uniformity, a single movement began to emerge. And the gradual disappearance of the more mystical, apocalyptic, and revo-lutionary groups meant that those elements were marginalized within the emerging tradition.

Further emigration east to Moravia and beyond continued the process of integration, even if the traditions each group brought with them sometimes led to disruption and division. It was in this region that Hutterite communities developed their distinctive expression of the Anabaptist tradition.

The Hutterites have practiced a common-purse form of commu-nity for almost all of the 475 years they have been in existence. As refugees from Austria, South Germany, and other areas of Europe, they found temporary relief from persecution in what is now the Czech Republic. Pooling their resources and living as interdependent communities may initially have been an emergency measure, but it soon became a hallmark of their spirituality and discipleship, rooted in their interpretation of the Bible and their understanding of the link between possessions and ultimate loyalties.

Persecution pursued these communities further east into Romania, Hungary, the Ukraine, and Russia, before they eventually found safety (if not wholehearted acceptance) in North America. The *Chronicle of the Hutterian Brethren* records their sufferings, struggles, and persistence in the face of external pressure and internal discord. It also sets out principles and practices that have guided their communities through the centuries.[14]

The multiple origins of the Anabaptist movement are still visible among contemporary Anabaptists in Europe, North America, and elsewhere. Cultural, linguistic, and ethnic factors still play a part, as do theological emphases and church traditions. Divisions over various issues have produced several denominations. Mennonites, Hutterites, and Amish may share a common heritage, but they disagree profoundly on how to interpret and embody this today.

Nevertheless, it is legitimate to speak of an Anabaptist movement, Anabaptist tradition, or Anabaptist vision. A famous attempt to describe this tradition was a speech by Mennonite historian Harold S. Bender in 1944, entitled "The Anabaptist Vision," in which he argued that the core elements were discipleship, brotherhood (or community), and nonresistance. Bender arrived at this conclusion by concentrating on the Swiss Brethren and Mennonites and excluding other groups he did not approve of, but this summary remains influential.[15] Subsequent writers have offered alternative proposals, influenced inevitably by their own context and convictions, and interpreting the historical data in different ways. One of the most influential interpretations is C. Arnold Snyder's magisterial *Anabaptist History and Theology*.[16]

Among the convictions widely shared by Anabaptists by the end of the sixteenth century were the following:

- Christians are to follow the example of Jesus and obey his teachings, whatever the consequences.
- The Bible is authoritative on ethical and ecclesial issues as well as theology.
- Church and state are both divinely ordained but are to be kept separate.

- Churches are communities of baptized disciples who are accountable to and for one another.

- Church discipline (including the use of the "ban") is crucial to maintain the purity and distinctiveness of the church.

- Followers of Jesus are to share their resources freely with one another.

- Nonviolence and truth telling are essential aspects of discipleship, so Christians should not fight or swear oaths.

- Suffering is normal for faithful disciples and is a mark of the true church.

Not all of these convictions were held by all first-generation Anabaptists, many of whom would also have emphasized the work of the Holy Spirit in the church, the necessity of interpreting Scripture together rather than individually, the urgency of evangelism, and the imminence of the return of Christ. Some groups, as we have noted, practiced community of goods rather than mutual aid. For others foot washing was an important component in their worship and community life. The evolving tradition abandoned certain elements, reinterpreted others, and emphasized what was regarded as essential.

Whatever diversity there may have been among early Anabaptists, the authorities were in no doubt that they were facing a single movement that represented a serious threat to both church and state. The number of people actively involved in this movement is difficult to ascertain, but it certainly ran into tens of thousands within the first generation. And many more people were attracted to Anabaptism but were not baptized as members, aware of what this step might cost them. Thousands of Anabaptists were martyred in the sixteenth century.

Scattered across Europe, the movement constituted only a tiny fraction of the population. But fear of Anabaptism was rife, even in England, where Anabaptist refugees were seized, imprisoned, and executed or deported before the movement could take hold. Anabaptist practices were explicitly repudiated in the *Thirty-Nine Articles* of the Church of England, and the accusation of being an "Anabaptist" was

used for centuries to discredit anyone regarded as theologically suspect or socially deviant. Even today, when many Christians in Britain
and Ireland gladly identify themselves as Anabaptists, this label can
still cause consternation in some circles.

ANABAPTISTS TODAY

Anabaptists today can be divided into four communities. First,
there are the descendants of the early Anabaptists: the Mennonites,
Amish, and Hutterites. Second, there are other denominations that
began later but drew inspiration from Anabaptism: various Brethren
groups, the Bruderhof movement, and some Baptists. Third, there
are new Anabaptist churches in many nations as a result of Mennonite and Brethren missionary activities. And fourth, there are neo-
Anabaptists, who belong to other traditions but acknowledge the
formative influence of Anabaptism.[17]

Each of these communities interprets the Anabaptist tradition in
its own way. Some have fixed views on most issues; others continue to
reflect on the contemporary application of the tradition. Newcomers—
new Anabaptists and neo-Anabaptists—may bring disturbing challenges as they interpret the tradition in surprising ways. *The Naked Anabaptist* makes no claim to be the only or most authentic interpretation
of the Anabaptist tradition. The core convictions on which this book is
based are simply an attempt by neo-Anabaptists in Britain and Ireland
to distill the essence of the Anabaptist tradition and apply its insights in
order to be more faithful followers of Jesus in our context.

Neo-Anabaptists are inspired especially by the first generation
of Anabaptists, which is why this chapter has concentrated on that
era. But there is much also to be learned from other Anabaptists
who through the centuries have interpreted the tradition in diverse
ways, and from other Anabaptist communities today.

Amish and Hutterites

Anabaptists in Britain and Ireland have had least contact with the
Amish, who are only marginally present here (there is a Beachy Amish
community in Southern Ireland). What we have learned from them
has come mainly from books we have read and stories we have heard.

Despite the huge cultural gap between us and the Amish, some of us have been attracted by their strong community ethos, challenged by their whole-life approach to discipleship, intrigued by discerning choices they have made in relation to technology and contemporary culture, and humbled by their capacity to forgive, demonstrated so powerfully in their response to the shooting of five of their children in the Nickel Mines tragedy in October 2006.[18]

But we are much less attracted by other aspects of Amish life and faith, some of which are evident also among the Hutterites. Their communities seem to be stuck in a cultural time warp, as they insist on conformity to a restrictive and outdated dress code, require women to be subservient to men, read out old sermons rather than preaching fresh ones, and question whether anyone outside their communities can truly be Christian (although in the final analysis they leave judgment on this issue to God).

We have had some contact with one branch of the Hutterites. I have on several occasions visited the Hutterian Bruderhof outside Robertsbridge in East Sussex, spending time with members of the community and learning about their way of life.[19] In 1993 the Anabaptist Network held its first residential conference there and deeply appreciated the hospitality of the community. We worked alongside them in their fields and workshops, shared their homes, ate with them, and participated in their worship. I have always experienced two competing reactions to these visits. On the one hand, I am relieved to leave a community that I find introverted, patriarchal, judgmental, and in thrall to ossified spiritual and cultural traditions. On the other hand, I feel the challenge of this whole-life approach to Christian discipleship and the attraction of being part of a counter-cultural community.

But if we are willing to look beyond less appealing features of the Hutterite and Amish traditions, we might recognize that these traditions challenge some of the powerful idols of our culture and question our collusion and compromises. In fact, we might discern some Anabaptist convictions and practices in their most naked and unadorned state. For instance,

- They regard all of life as sacred and reject the sacred/secular division that has afflicted Christians in most traditions through the centuries. They are committed to cultivating portions of the earth, as well as communities of Christian disciples, in preparation for the kingdom of God.

- They have rejected the widespread assumption among Christians that all but the most shameful professions are acceptable options and that Christians should be present in most workplaces. Instead, they have advised their members to avoid certain trades and occupations as incompatible with discipleship—not only those associated with warfare, but those that cater to human vanity and those that make money without actually producing anything useful.

- They need to be persuaded that the advantages of embracing new technology outweigh the disadvantages. These may make life easier, but they might diminish or destroy community, restrict opportunities for personal growth and discipleship, and require collusion with cultural values that clash with their convictions.

- The use of "casting lots" when choosing leaders may be unusual (although it also has biblical precedents) but indicates reluctance to assume that the community always knows what is best. Selecting candidates, but then inviting God to choose between them, challenges the desire to manage and control such processes.

- The Hutterite practice of sharing possessions in common not only has biblical precedent but is profoundly counter-cultural in societies where private property is foundational to the global economic system and the basis of personal ambition and anxiety.

- Despite sharp disputes, the pressure of living together in close proximity, painful divisions, and human frailties, the Hutterite community has remained committed to nonviolence and has never experienced a homicide.

Mennonites

Anabaptists in Britain and Ireland have had most contact with the

Mennonites, and it is to this branch of the movement that we owe the greatest debt. Many of us encountered Anabaptism through the work and witness of the London Mennonite Centre in Highgate, which for over fifty years has been a source of inspiration, a place of hospitality, a point of connection and conversation, and a resource center for anyone interested in exploring the Anabaptist tradition. Staff members and volunteers from the Mennonite community in North America have embodied this tradition and have shared its distinctive insights on discipleship, community, peace and justice, worship, spirituality, hospitality, and lifestyle. The Anabaptist Network began at the London Mennonite Centre and continues to have a close relationship with this community. Other Anabaptist-oriented groups make use of its facilities and encounter one another there.

Many years ago Mennonites decided not to plant churches in Britain and Ireland or try to establish a denominational presence there. This noncompetitive approach has enabled the London Mennonite Centre to serve a very wide constituency and has meant that Anabaptist values and insights have permeated many other traditions. However, it has also limited the scope for Anabaptist principles to be worked out at a congregational level. For many years, Wood Green Mennonite Church, a small congregation integrally connected to the London Mennonite Centre, has been the only Mennonite congregation in Britain.

While this book was being written, discussions have been taking place about the possibility of setting up an Anabaptist network of congregations, linking existing and emerging congregations in an informal network. Very few of these congregations will be explicitly Anabaptist or Mennonite, but they will support each other's attempts to work out Anabaptist principles in their various communities. The experience of Mennonite congregations elsewhere in the world will be an important resource for this network.

A number of us have visited North American Mennonite churches and seminaries, both to learn from these historic Anabaptist communities and to interpret to them the surprising resurgence of interest in their tradition in post-Christendom Europe. These transatlantic links have been very important to us. Some of us have also valued our connections with Mennonites in other parts of Europe—congregations that trace their history back to the sixteenth century and newer congregations planted by American Mennonite missionaries. And we are very grateful for the largely unheralded contributions of Mennonites to the Northern Ireland peace process.[20]

It has been the Mennonites (in North America, Europe, and Britain and Ireland) who have mediated the Anabaptist tradition to most of us. They have demonstrated how Anabaptist insights are worked out in the lives of families and congregations, and how this tradition can be passed on to the next generation. Sometimes we have been disappointed by what we have found in Mennonite circles—collusion with consumerism, conventional church services, cumbersome decision-making processes, and reluctance to share their faith with others. Our encounters with Mennonites have saved us from idealizing Anabaptism. But we deeply appreciate many aspects of the Mennonite tradition:

- The humility, gentleness, peacefulness, and commitment to simplicity that many Mennonites seem unconsciously to exhibit, embodying core Anabaptist values.

- The recovery of the maligned and neglected Anabaptist tradition through careful historical research and imaginative ways of telling this story.

- The tradition of hospitality that recognizes the crucial place of eating together in building and sustaining community.

- The persistent witness against war, capital punishment, and other forms of lethal violence.

- The peacemaking attitudes and skills that Mennonites have developed and refined over many years, offering realistic alternatives to coercion and discord in many areas of life.

- The commitment to practical discipleship, living out faith rather than talking too much about it, and following Jesus.

I will not become Hutterite, Amish, or Mennonite, but I am grateful that the principles of "naked Anabaptism" are sometimes clothed in Hutterite, Amish, and Mennonite dress, and I honor their attempts over many years to be faithful and radical followers of Jesus. The Anabaptist tradition has never been uniform. From the earliest years there were different emphases and divergent practices. Anabaptists today will interpret the Anabaptist vision in ways that make sense in our various cultures and contexts. But there are foundational insights, deep convictions, and enduring values that have shaped this tradition, for which the first Anabaptists were willing to die, and which all who accept the label "Anabaptist" recognize and want to embody.

8

Anabaptism Today

AS PROMISED at the end of chapter 6, and in the spirit of *The Naked Anabaptist*, we begin this final chapter by uncovering some of the weaknesses and limitations of the Anabaptist tradition. Beneath our clothes may be all kinds of blemishes and imperfections that we prefer to keep hidden from all but those closest to us. In fact, we may choose what we wear to mask or cover up unsightly aspects of our bodies and present ourselves in public as attractively as we can. Our intention in this chapter is to resist the temptation to cover up the blemishes in the Anabaptist tradition and to present it honestly and unguardedly.

Those who have contributed to this book, and many others, find the Anabaptist tradition attractive and inspiring, but we acknowledge that, like all Christian traditions, it has its shortcomings. Actually, one of the attractions of Anabaptist spirituality is its inherent humility and openness to correction and new insights,[1] so what follows can be understood as an Anabaptist approach to Anabaptism.

ANABAPTISM—WARTS AND ALL

Earlier chapters have revealed the deep fears the sixteenth-century movement provoked among its contemporaries and some of the charges brought against Anabaptists, past and present. While the worst excesses may have involved unrepresentative Anabaptists, the fears were not wholly unwarranted, nor are the charges without substance. We might want to deflect criticism by pointing out that the vast majority of Anabaptists have been honest, hard-working, peaceful, generous, humble, and hospitable; not given to taking part in naked processions or instituting reigns of terror. We might suggest their record stands in comparison with most other Christian traditions, especially in relation to violence against those they disagreed with. We might offer as an excuse the impact of persecution and the tendency of such pressure to lead to extremism and distortion. Or we might argue that the evolving tradition has corrected some of the imbalances of the heady early years and that Anabaptism today is more mature (if less radical).

But we want to listen to those who detect serious flaws in the Anabaptist tradition and are concerned that its growing influence might be unhelpful for Christians today. What have they uncovered?

Legalism

Any movement that takes discipleship as seriously as Anabaptists have and that determines to pay close attention to the text of Scripture rather than general ethical principles, is in danger of slipping into legalism. The sixteenth-century reformers were highly critical of the Anabaptists on this point, accusing them of "works-righteousness" and dubbing them "new monastics." The fundamental reformation principle of salvation by grace alone was, they believed, in danger of being undermined. And the accusation of legalism has been repeated through the centuries, especially when discipleship appears to be confused with cultural conservatism or legalism is equated with biblical literalism. It is likely that the pressure of persecution exacerbated this tendency: under pressure, groups often survive by maintaining strict discipline.[2] A persistent danger within the Anabaptist tradition has been for ethics to trump spirituality, so that discipleship is detached from the realm of grace. Some contemporary Anabaptists have expressed their own disquiet about this,[3] and it remains an area of concern.

Selectivity

Early Anabaptists criticized the reformers for being highly selective in their interpretation and application of biblical texts. Why, they asked, was Jesus normative for salvation but not for discipleship or patterns of church life? But the Anabaptist tradition can be criticized for a similar tendency (probably all Christian traditions can legitimately be accused of this). In particular, Anabaptists have been so concerned to listen to Jesus that they have often given the impression that the Old Testament is merely preparatory, not really worth engaging with on its own terms.

Frustrated by the ways in which their contemporaries were using Old Testament texts to countermand what they regarded as the clear teaching of Jesus on issues such as nonviolence, baptism, and swearing oaths, sixteenth-century Anabaptists adopted a Jesus-centered approach to Scripture. This was radical and liberating, an effective protest against what they perceived as misuse of the Old Testament, but it has left the Anabaptist tradition with an inadequate appreciation of the Old Testament. Furthermore, the danger of selectivity remains even for a tradition that claims to take Jesus seriously: Anabaptists have rarely engaged with the healing ministry of Jesus in the same way as they have attended to his ethical teaching.

Intellectualism/Anti-intellectualism

Through the centuries Anabaptists have often been accused of being anti-intellectual, denigrating scholarship and education, and of operating with an unsophisticated approach to the Bible and to theology. Once again, the legacy of the early years, when the universities were closed to them and their educated leaders were soon arrested and executed, may have played a significant role in this. Critics certainly dismissed as a counsel of necessity their confidence that all Christians, educated or not, were competent to interpret Scripture, with the help of the Holy Spirit.

So it is ironic that Anabaptists today are sometimes accused of being too intellectual. This is something the Anabaptist Network has struggled against. In our publications and conferences, we have not always been sufficiently down to earth in exploring the practical outworkings of our Anabaptist values and convictions. One of the reasons may be that the twentieth-century recovery of the Anabaptist vision owed so much to Mennonite scholars and that we have learned much from them. An ongoing challenge for Anabaptists today is to demonstrate the practical relevance of this historic tradition.

Divisiveness

Encouraging all Christians to take responsibility for interpreting Scripture may be liberating, but it is also dangerous. The reformers soon withdrew this liberty from their congregations, but the Anabaptists persisted with it. One of the results of the practice was division—within and between congregations—as interpreters reached different conclusions about the meaning and application of the texts. Anabaptism is certainly not the only tradition to be riddled by divisions since the breakup of Christendom in the sixteenth century. The proliferation of denominations and splitting of congregations, often over relatively minor issues, has been a blight on the Christian community. But Anabaptism has had more than its fair share of discord and division, and the practice of "banning" recalcitrant members has resulted in the mutual excommunicating of congregations as well as the exclusion of dissenting church members.

As representatives of a tradition that so strongly advocates reconciliation and enemy-loving, Anabaptists have been unduly contentious. Church discipline may never have involved physical (even lethal) violence, as it did for centuries in Catholic or Protestant territories, but the psychological violence involved could be considerable. A Mennonite friend comments that the reason Mennonites have specialized in conflict resolution is that they have so much conflict to resolve.

Separatism

Although the first Anabaptists had little opportunity to participate actively and constructively in a society that rejected their convictions and excluded them, when Anabaptists have found themselves in less oppressive contexts they have often struggled to embrace a different perspective on social engagement. Separatist instincts, endorsed by foundational documents like the "Schleitheim Confession," have been internalized. At its worst, Anabaptist separatism has conveyed disregard for wider society and concern only for the maintenance and survival of their own families and church communities. The deep concern of many early Anabaptists for economic reform and social justice has not been mediated to many of their descendants.

Increasing numbers of contemporary Anabaptists recognize and reject this separatist tendency, engaging creatively and courageously in the political, social, economic, and cultural arenas. But the commitment to being "counter-cultural" that permeates the Anabaptist movement can discourage partnership with others and preclude involvement in initiatives that may be regarded as less than ideal.

Quietism

The early Anabaptists were enthusiastic and vocal in sharing their faith with any who would listen to them, urging people to repent and become followers of Jesus. Their testimony, even as they were led to the stake, was so worrying to the authorities that tongue screws were used to silence them. But the pressure of persecution gradually convinced Anabaptists that keeping quiet about their faith was the only way to survive, and most adopted this stance (some even signed agreements exchanging vows of silence so as to be left in peace). They became known as "the quiet in the land."

While quietism was understandable in such contexts, like separatism it has become embedded in the Anabaptist tradition. Not speaking openly about one's faith is now defended by some Anabaptists as a mark of humility, rather than as a hangover from a history of repression. Their emphasis is on living out their faith, rather than talking about it. But this approach to bearing witness to Jesus Christ is seriously deficient in a post-Christendom culture that knows little of what Christians believe and lacks the tools to interpret the way we live.

Inertia

All movements tend to become institutionalized in time, and Anabaptism is no exception. The vibrant and radical missionary movement of the first generation gradually morphed into the settled denominational life of later generations. Apostles and prophets gave way to bishops and pastors. The commitment to pacifism degenerated into passivity. The passion to baptize converts and plant new churches faded. Exciting debates about the meaning of Scripture were superseded by settled and unquestionable interpretations.

As in other traditions, periodic renewal movements have galvanized the faithful, but historic Anabaptist denominations and con-

166 / THE NAKED ANABAPTIST

gregations today are often characterized by cultural conformity and inertia. One symptom of this is reluctance to allow leaders to lead and an often obsessive commitment to "good process," which ensures all opinions are voiced and all options considered, but reduces progress to a snail's pace. A Mennonite friend says that "process is the Mennonite drug of choice."

How serious are these defects in the Anabaptist tradition? Are they problematic enough to discourage further engagement with Anabaptism? Or are they simply reservations to be noted when drawing on this tradition? Are they any more worrying than the weaknesses of other traditions? And does it help to know that Anabaptists today are aware of these issues and are addressing them?

AFFIRMING ANABAPTISM

Obviously, members of the Anabaptist Network, including contributors to this book, have concluded that the Anabaptist tradition, despite its shortcomings, is worth learning from. So, it seems, do others. Some of us, and members of historic Anabaptist congregations, have been surprised recently to come across extraordinarily affirming appraisals of the Anabaptist tradition from representatives of other traditions. Brian McLaren, for example, a leading figure in the emerging church constituency, writes,

> More and more Christian leaders are beginning to realize that for the millions of young adults who have recently dropped out of church, Christianity is a failed religion. Why? Because it has specialized in dealing with "spiritual needs" to the exclusion of physical and social needs. It has focused on "me" and "my eternal destiny," but it has failed to address the dominant sociological and global realities of their lifetime: systemic injustice, poverty, and dysfunction. Shouldn't a message purporting to be the best news in the world be doing better than this? We need a form of Christian faith that is holistic, integral, and balanced, that speaks of God's grace to individuals and to societies and the planet as a whole. We so desperately need, as we move into this emerging culture, to learn to live a life of Christ instead of just going to church. Anabaptists know more about this than the rest of us and you (the Anabaptists) need to let your knowledge rub off on others.[4]

Tom Sine, respected futurist, member of Mustard Seed Associates, and author of *The New Conspirators*,[5] concurs that God is doing something new through a new generation that has a distinctly Anabaptist accent in these uncertain times.

> These young conspirators . . . invite all of us to embrace a more radical, whole-life faith and to create churches that are more outwardly focused in mission. As Jim Wallis has observed (yes, Jim Wallis and Sojourners are another example of Anabaptist influence), many of these young activists have turned away from the influences of the religious right to embrace a more biblically progressive agenda for social transformation. They are consistently much more committed to working for social justice, racial reconciliation, and caring for God's good creation than many of the churches from which they come. . . . These new Anabaptist conspirators . . . have the possibility of calling growing numbers of young people from outside the Anabaptist tradition to join a more biblically radical approach to life, faith and witness for peace, justice and creation care.[6]

Evangelical conference speaker and author Gregory Boyd, president of Christus Victor Ministries, says,

> There is a beautiful and powerful grassroots Kingdom movement arising all over the globe. Millions of people are abandoning the Christendom paradigm of the traditional Christian faith in order to become more authentic followers of Jesus. From the Emergent Church movement to the Urban Monastic Movement to a thousand other independent groups and movements, people are waking up to the truth that the Kingdom of God looks like Jesus and that the heart of Christianity is simply imitating him. Millions are waking up to the truth that followers of Jesus are called to love the unlovable, serve the oppressed, live in solidarity with the poor, proclaim Good News to the lost, and be willing to lay down our life for our enemies. Multitudes are waking up to the truth that the distinctive mark of the Kingdom is the complete rejection of all hatred and violence and the complete reliance on love and service of others, including our worst enemies. Masses of people are waking up to the truth that followers of Jesus aren't called to try to win the world by acquiring power *over* others but by exercising power *under* others—the power of self-sacrificial love.

What many who are being caught up in this movement lack is a sense of *tribal identity* and *historical rooting*, and many are looking for this. A central feature of postmodernity is the longing to "live in a story" that's bigger than oneself. Many, therefore, are looking for a tradition they can align with. The only tradition that embodies what this rising breed of Kingdom radicals is looking for is the Anabaptist tradition. This is the only tradition that consistently refused political power and violence. This is the only tradition that made humble, self-sacrificial love the centerpiece of what it means to follow Jesus. It's the only tradition that isn't soaked in blood and the only tradition that looks remotely like Jesus. Many (in fact, *most*) of the early leaders of this movement in the 16th century paid for their non-compliance with the Christendom paradigm by being martyred. This tradition is a treasure to be cherished. And it's a tradition whose time may have come, for this is precisely the vision of the Kingdom that millions today are waking up to.[7]

What these commentators are affirming is that, whatever its deficiencies, the Anabaptist tradition offers a place of belonging and a source of inspiration for Christians today as we face the challenges of a post-Christendom culture, in which the long-dominant forms of institutional Christianity are declining and struggling. Whether or not we may wish to be labeled "Anabaptist," this marginalized tradition offers a place to stand and a community from which to draw strength. Boyd is not the only one to wonder if Anabaptism is a "tradition whose time may have come"—not because it is unblemished or offers us all we need, but because it has a distinctive and unusual contribution to make.

Alan Kreider has suggested an analogy that expresses this idea. He invites us to imagine the varied Christian traditions as voices in a choir. Some of these voices have long been silent (or silenced), but there are signs that they are being heard once more.

Alternatively, we could think of instruments in an orchestra, each contributing in its own distinctive way to the music the whole orchestra is performing. The different instruments sound very different and participate in diverse ways, some more prominent at one time than another. Their interplay as well as their unique sounds enrich the performance.

For some time, though, the Anabaptist instrument has been missing or muted. This has not prevented the performance from continuing. Indeed, its long absence has often not even been noticed. But something has been lacking, and the performance is reaching a critical point, at which this missing instrument is needed as perhaps never before. It is not a solo instrument. It is simply one instrument in the orchestra. But the time has come for this instrument, confidently but with sensitivity and in harmony with the other instruments, to make its distinctive contribution.

This analogy is helpful, because it reinforces three things on which this book has insisted. First, the Anabaptist tradition is distinctive and potent. Second, it is not all-sufficient or without inadequacies. Third, it is one tradition among others and shares much in common with Christians in all other traditions. Those who identify with the Anabaptist tradition today recognize gratefully the huge contribution of many other Christian traditions. All we are proposing is that the marginalized Anabaptist tradition also has something to offer.

SPIRITUALITY AND DISCIPLESHIP
We have already indicated, using the Anabaptist Network's seven core convictions as a framework, many of the gifts Anabaptism can bring, especially to Christians in a post-Christendom society. But we recognize that these convictions are a work in progress and do not fully express the Anabaptist vision. Reflecting on them again while writing this book, I have become convinced that we will soon need to revise them once more as we continue to learn from the Anabaptist tradition.

Two aspects of the Anabaptist tradition about which more needs to be said are spirituality and discipleship. Although discipleship is mentioned three times in the core convictions, the distinctive nature of discipleship in the Anabaptist tradition is not spelled out. And, though it may be possible to deduce quite a bit from these convictions about Anabaptist spirituality, this is mentioned only once. But discipleship is at the heart of Anabaptism, and it is a distinctive Anabaptist spirituality that undergirds and nourishes discipleship in the Anabaptist tradition.

Actually, differentiating spirituality and discipleship in this way is probably illegitimate in all Christian traditions, but especially in relation to Anabaptism. For spirituality in the Anabaptist tradition is a "spirituality of discipleship." This is the implication of one of the most memorable and most frequently quoted of all sixteenth-century Anabaptist texts (already quoted in an earlier chapter): "No one can know Christ unless he follows after him in life . . . and no one can follow him unless he first knows him." True spirituality and discipleship cannot be separated.

During the past year, the Anabaptist study group that meets in my home has been reading together David Augsburger's *Dissident Discipleship*,[8] which spells out various aspects of discipleship in the Anabaptist tradition. We have explored the eight practices that he suggests are crucial to Anabaptist discipleship, including "habitual humility," "authentic witness," and "resolute nonviolence." We have yet to engage with the final chapter on "subversive spirituality," but it is already clear that these practices flow out of and are sustained by a particular understanding of spirituality. Augsburger defines this as "tripolar spirituality."

> Spirituality in the Anabaptist tradition is not "monopolar," concerned exclusively with a subjective encounter with one's inner self. Nor is it "bipolar," concerned to know God as well as oneself. Tripolar spirituality adds a third dimension—our engagement with other people. "The spirituality of personal transformation (the inner journey), the experience of divine encounter (the God-ward journey), and the relation of integrity and solidarity with the neighbor (the co-human journey with friend and enemy, with neighbor and persecutor) cannot be divided. Tripolar spirituality sees all three as interdependent.[9]

Early Anabaptists used the German term *Gelassenheit* to advocate this kind of tripolar spirituality. Medieval mystics had used this term to describe an attitude of detachment from the material world that would free the soul to seek after God, but the Anabaptists interpreted it holistically and applied it to many aspects of discipleship. *Gelassenheit* can be translated as "yieldedness." For Anabaptists this implied submission to the lordship of Christ, obedience to the teachings of Scripture, an inner attitude of renunciation matched by a readiness to suffer for one's faith, open-handed generosity with one's possessions, prayerful dependence on God, acceptance of community discipline, speaking truthfully regardless of the consequences, and refusal to defend oneself.

Tripolar spirituality, or *Gelassenheit*, is evident in Anabaptist understandings of the core Christian practices of baptism and communion. In the Anabaptist tradition, baptism is not only a public declaration of faith in Christ or an outward sign of an internal experience. It is also an invitation to the congregation to assume pastoral responsibility for the person being baptized and a commitment to submit to the discipline of the community in order to grow as a disciple. And when members of this community share bread and wine together, they not only examine their own hearts and give thanks to God. They also renew their commitment to one another—to share their resources and to be willing to lay down their lives for each other.

Gelassenheit is the spirituality of the "naked Anabaptist." It speaks of vulnerability and openness, an unguarded approach to life, recognizing one's weaknesses and frailties. It is also the discipleship of the "naked Anabaptist." It speaks of nonviolence, truth telling, and honesty, and the availability of one's resources to meet the needs of others. And because it renounces concerns about social achievements and impressing others, it is profoundly subversive, refusing to be overawed or cowed by those with power, wealth, or learning.[10] It is no coincidence that the practice of foot washing has been much more prevalent in Anabaptist communities than in most other traditions, for this symbolizes the spirit of *Gelassenheit* and calls members of the community back to this attitude and behavior. It is to such "yieldedness" that Anabaptists, and many other Christians in various traditions, through the centuries have aspired.[11]

ANABAPTISM TODAY

The Anabaptist tradition, then, is flawed and imperfect. Even at its best it needs to receive insights from other traditions to correct its imbalances. But many Christians today have found it inspirational and life-giving. Some suspect it might be a tradition whose time has come in post-Christendom western societies. Our hope is that *The Naked Anabaptist* will encourage others, who are not yet familiar with this tradition, to investigate it further.

Why? Not primarily so that the Anabaptist Network expands or the influence of the Anabaptist tradition spreads. Our interest is not in Anabaptism for its own sake, but in a tradition that helps us become more faithful followers of Jesus.

We pay tribute to generations of Anabaptist Christians who witnessed faithfully, refused to conform to social norms, pioneered new ways of being church, challenged dominant assumptions about violence, and sometimes suffered appallingly. We acknowledge, too, earlier dissenting movements, whose legacy is embodied in the Anabaptist tradition and whose courage and determination also inspire us. And some of us identify ourselves as "Anabaptist-minded," "Anabaptist-influenced," "Anabaptist-orientated," "hyphenated Anabaptists," or simply "Anabaptists" (although we are conscious of how much less costly this is today than often in the past). But we are interested in the Anabaptist tradition only as a means to an end. We find this tradition an unusually helpful lens through which to look at Scripture. It challenges and disturbs us as well as inspiring us, summoning us to wholehearted discipleship. And it keeps pointing us back to Jesus as the one we are to follow as well as worship.

Resources on Anabaptism

The Anabaptist Network, formed in 1991, is a relational network of individuals interested in learning from the Anabaptist tradition and from one another. Through publications, study groups, conferences, newsletters, resource houses, a theology forum, and a website, it offers resources to its members and others. Further information can be obtained by writing to the Anabaptist Network at 14 Shepherds Hill, London, N6 5AQ, or by sending an email to admin@anabaptistnetwork.com.

The Anabaptist Network is one of several organizations with Anabaptist-oriented values. Other groups are listed below in the websites section.

The longest-established Anabaptist community in Britain and Ireland is the London Mennonite Centre, which has the most extensive collection of Anabaptist books and other resources.

BOOKS
History of Anabaptism
Durnbaugh, Donald. *The Believers' Church.* Scottdale, Pa.: Herald Press, 1985.

Estep, William. *The Anabaptist Story.* Grand Rapids, Mich.: Eerdmans, 1996.

Goertz, Hans-Jürgen. *The Anabaptists.* London and New York: Routledge, 1996.

Klaassen, Walter. *Anabaptism in Outline*. Scottdale, Pa.: Herald Press, 1981.

Liechty, Daniel, ed. *Early Anabaptist Spirituality: Selected Writings*. New York: Paulist Press, 1994.

Murray, Stuart. *Biblical Interpretation in the Anabaptist Tradition*. Kitchener, Ont.: Pandora Press, 2000.

Pearse, Meic. *The Great Restoration: The Religious Radicals of the 16th and 17th Centuries*. Carlisle, U.K.: Paternoster, 1998.

Snyder, C. Arnold. *Anabaptist History and Theology*. Kitchener, Ont.: Pandora Press, 1995.

————. *From Anabaptist Seed*. Kitchener, Ont.: Pandora Press, 1999.

————, and Linda Huebert Hecht, eds. *Profiles of Anabaptist Women*, Waterloo, Ont.: Wilfrid Laurier University Press, 1996.

Williams, George. *The Radical Reformation*. Kirksville, Mo.: Sixteenth Century Journal Publishers, 1992.

Anabaptism Today

Augsburger, David. *Dissident Discipleship*. Grand Rapids, Mich.: Brazos, 2006.

Bartley, Jonathan. *Faith and Politics after Christendom*. Milton Keynes, U.K.: Paternoster, 2006.

Kraybill, Donald. *The Upside-Down Kingdom*. Scottdale, Pa.: Herald Press, 1990.

Kraybill, Nelson. *On the Pilgrim's Way*. Scottdale, Pa.: Herald Press, 1999.

Kreider, Alan, Eleanor Kreider, and Paulus Widjaja. *A Culture of Peace: God's Vision for the Church*. Intercourse, Pa.: Good Books, 2005.

Kreider, Alan, and Eleanor Kreider. *Worship and Mission after Christendom*. Milton Keynes, U.K.: Paternoster, 2009.

Kreider, Alan, and Stuart Murray. *Coming Home: Stories of Anabaptists in Britain and Ireland*. Kitchener, Ont.: Pandora Press, 2000.

Murray, Stuart. *Church after Christendom*. Milton Keynes, U.K.: Paternoster, 2005.

————. *Post-Christendom: Church and Mission in a Strange New World*. Carlisle, U.K.: Paternoster, 2004.

Pimlott, Jo, and Nigel Pimlott. *Youth Work after Christendom.* Milton Keynes, U.K.: Paternoster, 2008.

Roth, John. *Beliefs: Mennonite Faith and Practice.* Scottdale, Pa.: Herald Press, 2004.

———. *Practices: Mennonite Work and Worship.* Scottdale, Pa.: Herald Press, 2009.

———. *Stories: How Mennonite Came to Be.* Scottdale, Pa.: Herald Press, 2006.

Snyder, C. Arnold. *Following in the Footsteps of Christ.* London: Darton, Longman & Todd, 2004 / Maryknoll, N.Y.: Orbis, 2004.

Weaver, J. Denny. *Becoming Anabaptist.* Scottdale, Pa.: Herald Press, 2005.

Yoder, John Howard. *The Politics of Jesus.* Grand Rapids, Mich.: Eerdmans, 1993.

Devotional Resources

Take Our Moments and Our Days. Scottdale, Pa.: Herald Press, 2007. Compiled by several contributors, this is an Anabaptist prayer book in two volumes. The first volume contains morning and evening prayers for the period between Advent and Pentecost. The second volume provides a four-week cycle for the rest of the church year (so-called "ordinary time"). This focuses on the teaching and ministry of Jesus: the Lord's Prayer (week one), the Beatitudes (week two), Jesus' parables (week three), and Jesus' miracles (week four).

Kropf, Marlene, and Eddy Hall. *Praying with the Anabaptists: The Secret of Bearing Fruit.* Newton, Kan.: Faith and Life Press, 1994.

Snyder, C. Arnold, and Galen Peters, eds. *Reading the Anabaptist Bible.* Kitchener, Ont.: Pandora, 2002.

WEBSITES

www.anabaptistnetwork.com
the website of the Anabaptist Network, with information about the Network's activities and extensive resources on Anabaptism

www.postchristendom.com
the website that accompanies the After Christendom series published by Paternoster since 2004, with extracts from the books, summaries, study material, and a forum

www.urbanexpression.org.uk
> the website of Urban Expression, an inner-city mission agency with Anabaptist values

www.menno.org.uk
> the website of the London Mennonite Centre, incorporating Bridge Builders (conflict transformation) and Metanoia (book service)

www.ekklesia.co.uk
> the extensive website of the Christian political think tank Ekklesia, which is influenced by Anabaptist perspectives

www.workshop.org.uk
> the website of Workshop, a Christian training program that has introduced many people to Anabaptism

www.peacechurch.org.uk
> the website of a group of emerging churches, committed to peace and drawing on the Anabaptist tradition

www.cptuk.org.uk
> the website of the British branch of Christian Peacemaker Teams, an active peacemaking initiative in areas of conflict

www.gameo.org
> the Global Anabaptist Mennonite Encyclopedia Online, an enormous website with extensive resources on Anabaptism

www.aaanz.mennonite.net
> the website of the Anabaptist Association of Australia and New Zealand

http://anisa.org.za/
> the website of the emerging Anabaptist Network in South Africa

The Naked Anabaptist Study Guide

This short study guide is designed for small groups who have read *The Naked Anabaptist* or are reading it together.

CORE CONVICTION 1

Jesus is our example, teacher, friend, redeemer, and Lord. He is the source of our life, the central reference point for our faith and lifestyle, for our understanding of church and our engagement with society. We are committed to following Jesus as well as worshipping him.

1. "Example, teacher, friend, redeemer, Lord": with which of these designations of Jesus do you *least* identify? How might you explore this further?

2. What examples can you give of Jesus being "the central reference point" for your life or your church? What examples can you give of him *not* being this?

3. Do you agree that in many places Jesus is worshipped but not followed? What are the implications of this?

4. Hans Denck wrote, "No one can know Christ unless he follows after him in life." Do you agree? Or is this a return to "salvation by works"?

5. How do you respond to the proposal that we should drop the term *Christians* and call ourselves "followers of Jesus"?

CORE CONVICTION 2

Jesus is the focal point of God's revelation. We are committed to a Jesus-centered approach to the Bible and to the community of faith as the primary context in which we read the Bible and discern and apply its implications for discipleship.

1. Does a "Jesus-centered approach to the Bible" inevitably mean that parts of Scripture are downgraded?

2. Think about Bible studies you have participated in. Have these avoided "the pooling of ignorance"? How can Christians be resourced to discern and apply the implications of the Bible?

3. How can churches resist the default dominance of monologue sermons? Or should they even try?

4. What practical strategies can you suggest to ensure that biblical interpretation does not get stuck but leads on to application and discipleship?

5. Try out the practice of "dwelling in the Word." Choose a biblical passage and give each person a copy of it. Read the passage aloud, and then allow a period of quiet reflection. Share with another person what struck you, and listen to his reflection. Then tell the rest of the group what your reflection partner noticed (not what you noticed).

CORE CONVICTION 3

Western culture is slowly emerging from the Christendom era when church and state jointly presided over a society in which almost all were assumed to be Christian. Whatever its positive contributions on values and institutions, Christendom seriously distorted the gospel, marginalized Jesus, and has left the churches ill equipped for mission in a post-Christendom culture. As we reflect on this, we are committed to learning from the experience and perspectives of movements such as Anabaptism that rejected standard Christendom assumptions and pursued alternative ways of thinking and behaving.

1. How much evidence can you find that your community is in post-Christendom?

2. Are Anabaptists too hung up on Christendom—unable to appreciate its huge benefits and locked into an unhelpful Christendom/post-Christendom framework?

3. What "alternative ways of thinking and behaving" does the Anabaptist tradition offer? How might you learn from these?

4. How might you access the insights of other marginalized movements and check out whether they shared Anabaptist perspectives?

5. How helpful do you find the analogy of exile in describing the situation of the church in the West? Are there other helpful motifs we could use?

CORE CONVICTION 4

The frequent association of the church with status, wealth, and force is inappropriate for followers of Jesus and damages our witness. We are committed to vulnerability and to exploring ways of being good news to the poor, powerless, and persecuted, aware that such discipleship may attract opposition, resulting in suffering and sometimes ultimately martyrdom.

1. How can Christians avoid becoming associated with status and wealth if the gospel is effective in a society and wins many adherents? Should they try to avoid this?

2. In what ways does "association with status, wealth, and force" damage the witness of followers of Jesus?

3. What examples can you give of ways in which you or others have been "good news to the poor"?

4. What opportunities are available to a church on the margins that were not possible for a dominant church?

5. How do western Christians engage with 2 Timothy 3:12?

CORE CONVICTION 5

Churches are called to be committed communities of discipleship and mission, places of friendship, mutual accountability, and multivoiced worship. As we eat together, sharing bread and wine, we sustain hope as we seek God's kingdom together. We are committed to nurturing and developing such churches, in which young and old are valued, leadership is consultative, roles are related to gifts rather than gender, and baptism is for believers.

1. Is it realistic in contemporary culture to practice mutual admonition? How would a church go about introducing this practice?

2. What role do eating and hospitality play in your Christian experience? How might you explore these practices in new ways?

3. How can your community find a healthy balance between consultation and leadership?

4. What kinds of people in your experience are in the greatest danger of being excluded? How can their voices be heard?

5. What difference would it make to your church if Hubmaier's "pledge of love" was used regularly and thoughtfully when you share bread and wine?

CORE CONVICTION 6

Spirituality and economics are interconnected. In an individualist and consumerist culture and in a world where economic injustice is rife, we are committed to finding ways of living simply, sharing generously, caring for creation, and working for justice.

1. What difference does it make whether we are motivated by charity or justice in our use of our resources?

2. Read Acts 2:42-47 and 4:32-37. Were those Anabaptist right who found here a biblical mandate for common-purse community?

3. How in practice do spirituality and economics interconnect? Which has the greater influence on the other?

4. What might you do to resist the influence of individualism and consumerism on your own life?

5. What are the problems with the contemporary practice of tithing in many churches?

CORE CONVICTION 7

Peace is at the heart of the gospel. As followers of Jesus in a divided and violent world, we are committed to finding nonviolent alternatives and to learning how to make peace between individuals, within and among churches, in society, and between nations.

1. Do you agree that "peace is at the heart of the gospel"? If not, how important is peace in relation to the gospel?

2. Is the just war approach still applicable in the context of modern warfare? If it were applied, what difference would it make?

3. Is it important that advocates of nonviolence should be able to demonstrate that this approach is effective?

4. What peace initiatives are you involved in, or might you get involved in?

5. "Let the Christians of the world agree that they will not kill each other." How do you respond to this "modest proposal for peace"?

AND FINALLY . . .

1. What aspects of the Anabaptist tradition do you find inspirational or challenging?

2. How might you respond to these?

3. What aspects of the Anabaptist tradition do you find least attractive? Why?

4. What topics in *The Naked Anabaptist* do you want to explore further? How will you do this?

Notes

INTRODUCTION

1. See www.anabaptistnetwork.com.

2. Alan Kreider and Stuart Murray, eds., *Coming Home: Stories of Anabaptists in Britain and Ireland* (Waterloo, Ont.: Pandora Press, 2000), 211-13.

3. See further in chapter 8.

4. See www.menno.org.uk.

5. Stuart Murray, *Post-Christendom: Church and Mission in a Strange New World* (Carlisle, U.K.: Paternoster, 2004).

CHAPTER 1

1. Duane Ruth-Heffelbower, *The Anabaptists Are Back!* (Scottdale, Pa.: Herald Press, 1991).

2. Alan Kreider and Stuart Murray, eds., *Coming Home: Stories of Anabaptists in Britain and Ireland* (Waterloo, Ont.: Pandora Press, 2000).

3. See www.postchristendom.com.

4. See www.aaanz.mennonite.net.

5. See www.churchcommunities.com.

6. See www.cpt.org.

7. See www.urbanexpression.org.uk.

8. See www.cruciblecourse.org.uk.

9. See www.menno.org.uk/bridgebuilders.

10. See www.metanoiabooks.org.uk.

11. See www.workshop.org.uk.

12. See www.ekklesia.co.uk.

13. See www.speak.org.uk.

14. This will be examined further in chapter 6.

15. Brian McLaren, *A Generous Orthodoxy* (Grand Rapids, Mich.: Zondervan, 2004).

16. In the foreword to David Greiser and Michael King, *Anabaptist Preaching* (Telford, Pa.: Cascadia, 2003), 9.

17. See http://www.mennoweekly.org/2008/4/21/author-connects-anabaptist-and-emergent-movements/.

18. For example, Stanley Hauerwas, *The Peaceable Kingdom* (London: SCM, 2003); James McClendon, *Systematic Theology I: Ethics* (Nashville: Abingdon, 1986); John Howard Yoder, *The Politics of Jesus* (Grand Rapids, Mich.: Eerdmans, 1993).

19. Doris Janzen Longacre, *More-with-Less Cookbook* (Scottdale, Pa.: Herald Press, 2003).

20. See further www.vorp.org.

21. This issue will be explored further in chapter 5.

22. A term popularized by Stanley Hauerwas and a translation of a Greek term in 1 Peter 1:1.

23. This will be explored further in chapter 6.

CHAPTER 2

1. We are glad that the term *naked* also implies "unguarded" and "vulnerable." The following chapters will indicate areas in which the Anabaptist tradition has blemishes and will attempt to be nondefensive about these.

2. These core convictions can be found at www.anabaptistnetwork. com/coreconvictions, where there is also a study guide and brief articles unpacking each conviction.

3. For a more complete and global list of Anabaptist convictions, see Alfred Neufeld, *What We Believe Together, Exploring the "Shared Convictions" of Anabaptist-Related Churches* (Intercourse, Pa.: Good Books, 2008).

4. The version used here was produced in January 2006 in light of discussions at our residential conference six months earlier.

5. Nigel Wright, "Spirituality as Discipleship: The Anabaptist Tradition," in Paul Fiddes, ed., *Under the Rule of Christ: Dimensions of Baptist Spirituality* (Oxford: Regent's Park College, 2008), 89-90.

CHAPTER 3

1. C. Arnold Snyder, *Following in the Footsteps of Christ* (London: Darton, Longman & Todd, 2004).

2. For further details, see Stuart Murray, *Post-Christendom: Church and Mission in a Strange New World* (Carlisle, U.K.: Paternoster, 2004), chapter 4.

3. Quoted in Gerhard Ebeling, *Luther* (London: Collins, 1972), 131.

4. John Howard Yoder, *The Politics of Jesus* (Grand Rapids, Mich.:

Eerdmans, 1993); Donald Kraybill, *The Upside Down Kingdom* (Scottdale, Pa.: Herald Press, 1990); Marcus Borg and Tom Wright, *The Meaning of Jesus: Two Visions* (London: SPCK, 1999); Brian McLaren, *The Secret Message of Jesus* (Nashville: Word, 2006); Walter Wink, *Engaging the Powers* (Minneapolis: Fortress, 1992); Shane Claiborne and Chris Haw, *Jesus for President* (Grand Rapids, Mich.: Zondervan, 2008); Steve Chalke and Alan Mann, *The Lost Message of Jesus* (Grand Rapids, Mich.: Zondervan, 2003); Michael Frost and Alan Hirsch, *ReJesus: A Wild Messiah for a Missional Church* (Peabody, Mass.: Hendrickson, 2009).

5. Eddie Gibbs and Ryan Bolger, *Emerging Churches* (Grand Rapids, Mich.: Baker, 2005), 44.

6. John Drane, *After McDonaldization* (London: Darton, Longman & Todd, 2008), 49, 121.

7. Walter Klaassen, *Anabaptism in Outline* (Scottdale, Pa.: Herald Press, 1981), 87. Chapter 7 will introduce Hans Denck.

8. In *Against the Terrible Errors of the Anabaptists* (1582).

9. For a much more detailed study, see Stuart Murray, *Biblical Interpretation in the Anabaptist Tradition* (Waterloo, Ont.: Pandora, 2000).

10. See further, Lloyd Pietersen, *Reading the Bible after Christendom* (Milton Keynes, U.K.: Paternoster, forthcoming).

11. Liberation theology is a predominantly Catholic movement that began in the 1960s and has had a worldwide impact through its writings and the practices of the "base ecclesial communities" in Brazil and elsewhere.

12. See Paul Peachey and Shem Peachey, "Answer of Some Who Are Called (Ana)baptists: Why They Do Not Attend the Churches: A Swiss Brethren Tract," *Mennonite Quarterly Review* 45 (January 1971), 5-32.

13. See http://interactivepreaching.net.

CHAPTER 4

1. See further Philip Jenkins, *The Lost History of Christianity* (Oxford: Lion, 2008).

2. The Lutheran Church in Sweden was disestablished in 2000. There is growing agitation for the Church of England to be disestablished, following the example of the Church in Wales.

3. This anecdote appears in Philip Jenkins, *God's Continent* (Oxford: Oxford University Press, 2007), 37.

4. The frequent reference to "western Christians" is necessary. Post-Christendom is not the context in which Christians in many parts of the world find themselves. The center of gravity of the global church is not

in Europe or North America now, but in regions where there has been no Christendom era. Anabaptists can be found in these areas too, but it is the contribution of the Anabaptist tradition to post-Christendom western Christians that is the focus of this chapter.

5. Even if you think the Christendom shift was necessary and appropriate, despite the disturbing features of the system which emerged, the Christendom era is over. It is time to move on.

6. Stuart Murray, *Post-Christendom: Church and Mission in a Strange New World* (Carlisle, U.K.: Paternoster, 2004), 19.

7. Murray, *Post-Christendom: Church and Mission in a Strange New World*, 20.

8. See Philip Jenkins, *The Next Christendom* (Oxford: Oxford University Press, 2002).

9. See www.urbanexpression.org.uk/convictions/commitments.

10. See further www.speak.org.uk

CHAPTER 5

1. See further www.freshexpressions.org.uk; www.emergingchurch.info; Stuart Murray, *Church after Christendom* (Milton Keynes, U.K.: Paternoster, 2005); Michael Moynagh, *emergingchurch.intro* (Oxford: Monarch, 2004); Michael Frost and Alan Hirsch, *The Shaping of Things to Come* (Peabody, Mass.: Hendrickson, 2004), and many other resources.

2. On these various proposals, see www.simplechurch.co.uk; James Thwaites, *The Church beyond the Congregation* (Carlisle, U.K.: Paternoster, 1999); Pete Ward, *Liquid Church* (Peabody, Mass.: Hendrickson/Carlisle, U.K.: Paternoster, 2002); and www.newmonasticism.org.

3. See, for example, Wolfgang Capito's criticisms as recorded in John Howard Yoder, ed., *The Legacy of Michael Sattler* (Scottdale, Pa.: Herald Press, 1973), 87; Ulrich Zwingli's concerns in his *Of Baptism*, in G. W. Bromiley, ed., *Zwingli and Bullinger* (London: SCM Press, 1953), 148; and Martin Luther in the preface to his commentary on the Sermon on the Mount.

4. See www.peacechurch.org.uk.

5. See Russell Snyder-Penner, "Hans Nadler's Oral Exposition of the Lord's Prayer," *Mennonite Quarterly Review* 65 (October 1991), 393-406.

6. This story also appears in Murray, *Church after Christendom*, 9.

7. See Paul Hiebert, *Missions and the Renewal of the Church* (Pasadena, Calif.: Fuller, 1983) and *Anthropological Reflections on Missiological Issues* (Grand Rapids, Mich.: Baker, 1994).

8. See Paul Peachey and Shem Peachey, "Answer of Some Who Are Called

(Ana)baptists: Why They Do Not Attend the Churches: A Swiss Brethren Tract," *Mennonite Quarterly Review* 45 (January 1971), 7.

9. See further C. Arnold Snyder and Linda Huebert Hecht, eds., *Profiles of Anabaptist Women: Sixteenth-century reforming pioneers* (Waterloo, Ont.: Wilfrid Laurier University Press, 1996).

10. And an issue on which there has been some convergence in recent years as representatives of different traditions have learned to appreciate and honor each other's perspectives on baptism.

11. H. Wayne Pipkin and John Howard Yoder, eds., *Balthasar Hubmaier: Theologian of Anabaptism* (Scottdale, Pa.: Herald Press, 1989), 393-408. See further Eleanor Kreider, *Given for You: A Fresh Look at Communion* (Leicester, U.K.: IVP, 1998).

CHAPTER 6

1. The next chapter gives more details of this movement and its relationship to Anabaptism.

2. Classic texts are Isaiah 1:11-17 and 58:1-14.

3. On this and other aspects of the economics of the Christendom system, see Stuart Murray, *Beyond Tithing* (Carlisle, U.K.: Paternoster, 2000).

4. The next chapter gives more details of this episode in early Anabaptist history.

5. Other common-purse communities, such as the short-lived Diggers in seventeenth-century England, seem not to have drawn on Anabaptism.

6. See Kim Tan, *The Jubilee Gospel* (Milton Keynes, U.K.: Authentic, 2008).

7. See www.ecocongregation.org.

8. See, for example, James Krabill, David Shenk, and Linford Stutzman, *Anabaptists Meeting Muslims* (Scottdale, Pa.: Herald Press, 2005).

9. See further Alan Kreider, Eleanor Kreider, and Paulus Widjaja, *A Culture of Peace: God's Vision for the Church* (Intercourse, Pa.: Good Books, 2005).

10. A good introduction to this issue is John Roth, *Choosing Against War* (Intercourse, Pa.: Good Books, 2002).

11. See www.cptuk.org.uk and Kathleen Kern, *In Harm's Way: A History of Christian Peacemaker Teams* (Eugene, Ore.: Cascade, 2008).

12. See www.menno.org.uk/bridgebuilders.

13. See www.vorp.com and Howard Zehr, *Changing Lenses: A New Focus for Crime and Justice* (Scottdale, Pa.: Herald Press, 2005).

14. Restorative justice practices have been adopted within the criminal

justice system in several nations (especially but not exclusively in the youth offending context), often alongside the existing system.

15. See Walter Wink, *Engaging the Powers: Discernment and Resistance in a World of Domination* (Minneapolis: Fortress Press, 1992).

CHAPTER 7

1. Examples mentioned in chapter 4 are the Waldensians, the Lollards, the Czech Brethren, the Moravians, and the early Baptists.

2. An excellent survey of this movement is Tom Scott and Robert Scribner, eds., *The German Peasants' War* (New Jersey: Humanities Press, 1991). To trace the links with Anabaptism, see James Stayer, *The German Peasants' War and Anabaptist Community of Goods* (Montreal/Kingston: McGill-Queen's University Press, 1991).

3. See www.anabaptistnetwork.com/schleitheimconfession.

4. For a more detailed account of this period, see C. Arnold Snyder, "The Birth and Evolution of Swiss Anabaptism, 1520–1530," *Mennonite Quarterly Review* 80 (October 2006), 501-645.

5. The stories of Margaret Hellwart and many other Anabaptist women are told in C. Arnold Snyder and Linda Huebert Hecht, eds., *Profiles of Anabaptist Women* (Waterloo, Ont.: Wilfrid Laurier University Press, 1996).

6. The classic study is Werner Packull, *Mysticism and the Early South German-Austrian Anabaptist Movement* (Scottdale, Pa.: Herald Press, 1977).

7. See further Walter Klaassen and William Klassen, *Marpeck: A Life of Dissent and Conformity* (Scottdale, Pa.: Herald Press, 2008).

8. Thieleman Van Braght, *Martyrs Mirror* (Scottdale, Pa.: Herald Press, 1950).

9. "Spiritualists" were uninterested in debates about forms and structures, convinced that spiritual experience was the only important concern.

10. See further Klaus Deppermann, *Melchior Hoffman* (Edinburgh, Scotland: T & T Clark, 1987).

11. For a popular account of this incident, see Anthony Arthur, *The Tailor King: The Rise and Fall of the Anabaptist Kingdom of Münster* (New York: St. Martin's Press, 1999).

12. See further Cornelius Krahn, *Dutch Anabaptism* (The Hague, The Netherlands: Martinus Nijhoff, 1968).

13. In Amsterdam, the early English Baptists, refugees from persecution in England, enjoyed the hospitality and support of Mennonites in the first decade of the seventeenth century.

14. *Chronicle of the Hutterian Brethren* (Rifton, N.Y.: Plough Publishing

House, 1987). For further information on the Hutterites, see John Hostetler, *Hutterite Society* (Baltimore: John Hopkins University Press, 1974) and Werner Packull, *Hutterite Beginnings* (Baltimore: John Hopkins University Press, 1995).

15. Harold S. Bender, *The Anabaptist Vision* (Scottdale, Pa.: Herald Press, 1944).

16. C. Arnold Snyder, *Anabaptist History and Theology* (Kitchener, Ont.: Pandora Press, 1995). See also his very accessible *Following in the Footsteps of Christ* (London: Darton, Longman & Todd, 2004).

17. For an introduction to several of these groups, see Donald Kraybill, *Who Are the Anabaptists? Amish, Brethren, Hutterites, and Mennonites* (Scottdale, Pa.: Herald Press, 2003).

18. For an introduction to the Amish, see Donald Kraybill, *The Riddle of Amish Culture* (Baltimore: John Hopkins University Press, 1989). On the Nickel Mines incident, see Donald Kraybill, et al., *Amish Grace: How Forgiveness Transcended Tragedy* (San Francisco: Jossey-Bass, 2007).

19. The Bruderhof movement began in Germany between the two World Wars and has been associated with the historic Hutterite movement (although they are not currently emphasizing this connection). See further www.churchcommunities.com.

20. See Joseph Liechty, "Mennonites and Conflict in Northern Ireland, 1970–1998," in Cynthia Sampson and John Paul Lederach, eds., *From the Ground Up: Mennonite Contributions to International Peacebuilding* (Oxford: Oxford University Press, 2000).

CHAPTER 8

1. Unlike their Catholic and Protestant contemporaries, sixteenth-century Anabaptist writers consistently invited their readers to challenge and correct them if they had better insights into Scripture.

2. Early Anabaptist communities that were less rigid (such as those associated with Marpeck and Denck) did not survive.

3. An influential example was Stephen Dintaman's article, "The Spiritual Poverty of the Anabaptist Vision," *The Conrad Grebel Review* 10 (Spring 1992), 205-8.

4. See http://www.mennoweekly.org/2008/4/21/author-connects-anabaptist-and-emergent-movements/.

5. Tom Sine, *The New Conspirators* (Milton Keynes, U.K.: Paternoster, 2008).

6. Tom Sine, "Joining the Anabaptist Conspirators," *The Mennonite*, June 3, 2008, 12-13.

7. Greg Boyd, addressing a Mennonite gathering in Pittsburgh, January 2009.

8. David Augsburger, *Dissident Discipleship* (Grand Rapids, Mich.: Brazos, 2006).

9. Augsburger, *Dissident*, 13.

10. This attitude, so irritating to the authorities, is evident throughout the accounts in *Martyrs Mirror*, as unlearned Anabaptists debated unapologetically with theologians, clergy, and inquisitors.

11. An obvious example is Francis of Assisi, whose spirituality of discipleship has much in common with the Anabaptist tradition, and who spoke of "naked, following the naked Christ."

The Author

Stuart Murray spent twelve years as an urban church planter in Tower Hamlets (East London) and has continued to be involved in church planting since then as a trainer, mentor, writer, strategist, and consultant.

For nine years he was Oasis Director of Church Planting and Evangelism at Spurgeon's College, London; he continues as an associate lecturer at the college.

He is chair of the Anabaptist Network and has a PhD in Anabaptist hermeneutics. Since September 2001, Stuart has worked under the auspices of the Anabaptist Network as a trainer and consultant, with particular interest in urban mission, church planting, and emerging forms of church.

Stuart is the founder of Urban Expression, a pioneering urban church-planting agency with teams in London, Glasgow, Manchester, Bristol, Birmingham, Stoke-on-Trent, and the Netherlands. There is now an Urban Expression in North America as well.

He has written several books on church planting, urban mission, emerging church, the challenge of post-Christendom, and the contribution of the Anabaptist tradition to contemporary missiology. Recent publications include *Post-Christendom: Church and Mission in a Strange New World* (Paternoster 2004), *Church after Christendom* (Paternoster 2005), and *Changing Mission* (CTBI 2006).

Stuart is married to Sian, a tutor at the Baptist College in Bristol, where they live. He has two grown sons and a grandson.